Developing Essential Literacy Skills

A Continuum of Lessons for Grades K–3

Robin Cohen

INTERNATIONAL
Reading Association
800 BARKSDALE ROAD, PO BOX 8139
NEWARK, DE 19714-8139, USA
www.reading.org

The International Reading Association attempts, through its publications, to provide a forum for a wide spectrum of opinions on reading. This policy permits divergent viewpoints without implying the endorsement of the Association.

Executive Editor, Books   Corinne M. Mooney
Developmental Editor   Charlene M. Nichols
Developmental Editor   Tori Mello Bachman
Developmental Editor   Stacey Lynn Sharp
Editorial Production Manager   Shannon T. Fortner
Design and Composition Manager   Anette Schuetz

Project Editors   Tori Mello Bachman and Rebecca A. Fetterolf

Cover   Design, Lise Holliker Dykes; Photograph © BananaStock

The publisher would appreciate notification where errors occur so that they may be corrected in subsequent printings and/or editions.

Library of Congress Cataloging-in-Publication Data

Cohen, Robin, 1946-
  Developing essential literacy skills : a continuum of lessons for
grades K-3 / Robin Cohen.
      p. cm.
  Includes bibliographical references and index.
  ISBN 978-0-87207-607-5
  1. Language arts (Primary) 2. Lesson planning. I. Title.
  LB1528.C63 2008
  372.6--dc22
                                                                    2008002169

To all the present and all the future Cohens and McCabes in my life—
Arnie, Jess, Rory, Russ, Jen, Marty, Kyle, Zachary, Raya,
and…

CONTENTS

ABOUT THE AUTHOR

Robin Cohen is a retired literacy specialist who works as an independent literacy consultant in U.S. school districts nationwide. She is also a writer and content advisor for Schoolwide, Inc., working on their newly developed Testing Fundamentals program. Robin worked in the New York City public schools for many years where she taught kindergarten and grades 1 and 2 before becoming a reading teacher. Most recently she worked at Liberty Elementary School located in Rockland County, New York. At Liberty she taught reading and served as a staff developer at all elementary-grade levels. Robin also served as an adjunct literacy professor at Saint Thomas Aquinas College in Sparkill, New York.

Robin has been invited to present workshops and seminars at numerous schools districts and conferences, most notably at the New York State Reading Conference teacher sessions and twice as the featured speaker at the New York State Reading Association's (NYSRA) Parent's Day Conference.

Robin has been the recipient of numerous literacy grant awards, most notably the Unsung Heroes in Education Award sponsored by Northern Life Insurance Company and grants sponsored by the New York City Teachers Consortium. One of these grants allowed Robin to establish a children's bookstore at P.S. 121 in the Bronx, where she was teaching at the time. The idea behind the bookstore project was to allow elementary students to buy and own quality children's literature at an affordable price. Robin published an article about the success of this project in *American Educator* magazine, a publication of the American Federation of Teachers. Interest in this project prompted an article in *Parade* magazine and led to the establishment of numerous children's bookstores in schools nationwide.

Robin has been fortunate to be a part of several prestigious awards granted to Liberty Elementary School. Liberty was a National Blue Ribbon School, was the first northeast school to receive the National School Change Award, and most recently was awarded the International Reading Association's Exemplary Reading Program Award for New York State.

Robin received the Friends of Literacy Award sponsored by NYSRA, was recognized as an Educator of Excellence by the National Council of Teachers of English, and was chosen New York State Reading Teacher of the Year for 2002–2003.

Robin is the proud parent of her three children, Jess, Russ, and Jenny, who are the founders of Schoolwide, Inc.

When not working, Robin and her husband, Arnie, spend as much time as they can with their three grandchildren, Kyle, Zach, and Raya, and are eagerly awaiting the arrival of their fourth grandchild in the spring.

Author Information for Correspondence and Workshops

Please feel free to contact the author with comments and questions about this book. Robin's e-mail address is arnrob@optonline.net.

ACKNOWLEDGMENTS

I thank all the incredible teachers who shared their wisdom about the importance of what is essential to the teaching of literacy and its place alongside test preparation for mastery examinations. This core group of teachers includes Lisa Madden, Allison Clancy, Carol Russell, Patricia Doherty, Joan Golden, Linda Cardinali, Marty McCabe, Irene Schlanger, Francisca White, and Anne Jacobs. I would also like to thank all the other Liberty Elementary School teachers at all grade levels and other assignments, such as Jim Grasso, the speech and language specialist, and Karen Andreasen, the English as a second language teacher, who participated in our numerous study groups over the past years in order to learn and grow as professionals. The lively and informative conversations we had in these groups allowed me to broaden my perspective about the teaching and learning happening inside and outside of your classrooms. I also want to give special thanks to Diane Smith and Sandy Connolly for being the original "Guinea pig" classroom; to my roommates Amelia McCafferty, my teaching assistant at Liberty, for being the person she is and for all she did above and beyond her required duties and Anne Jacobs for her quiet patience and her dedication to her students at Liberty. I also need to give special thanks to the other dedicated teaching assistants who are only assistants by title but are truly teachers by heart. Thanks to Pat Jacobson, literacy specialist and friend, who is always there for me and never says no, and to Alice Blueglass, principal extraordinaire for her love of children, for supporting all of our learning, and for always finding a way to make it work. You are an amazing group of educators as well as an amazing group of friends.

I need to thank Meryl Natelli and Virginia Fiore, my former principals at P.S. 121 in the Bronx, and Lesley Gordon, the former District 11 Early Childhood Coordinator, for pushing me to learn and grow. These women saw what was possible and allowed me to go there. I need to thank the amazing teachers like Pat McQueen, Jean Czarniecki, Veray Darby, Cathy Kelly, Linda Pappalardo, Cera Northern, and so many others at P.S. 121 who traveled the road by my side.

Special thanks go to several people who helped me through the adventure of writing this book: Rory Freed-Cohen for her extensive knowledge of literacy learning and of children's literature and for not only being a colleague and a daughter-in-law but more importantly for being my friend; Dr. Michael Shaw for his research knowledge, for his unending patience, for the time he took from his busy schedule to meet with me and talk me through the hard parts, and mostly for his friendship; Paul Eckstein, a true friend, without whose expertise, coaching, and calming my nerves, I might have given up on this manuscript; and Shelley Karlen for her unending support of this project. Also, I thank Corinne Mooney and Daniel Mangan on the editorial staff of the International Reading Association for their strong support of this manuscript and their help when I needed it. Thanks also to my editor, Tori Bachman, for holding my hand through this process and for her sense of humor and to my production editor, Becky Fetterolf, for helping me pull the whole thing together.

In addition I need to thank my children, Jess, Russ, Jen, Rory, and Marty, for loving me, advising me, and listening to me talk about this for weeks on end and my husband, Arnie, who made sure the house was clean, made sure that I ate, kept me calm, and gave support—not just during the writing of this book but throughout all our years together.

Finally, I would like to acknowledge Sharon Thomas, master teacher and friend, who kept pushing me for years by saying, "So, when are you going to write your book?" Well, Sharon, here it is!

CHAPTER 1

Creating an Essential Skills Continuum for Primary Grades

Research has identified the skills of phonemic awareness, phonics, fluency, vocabulary, and comprehension as crucial to the attainment of early reading abilities (National Institute of Child Health and Human Development [NICHD], 2000). These skills should be included in all comprehensive, developmentally appropriate language arts curricula developed by state education departments. The language arts curricula should also be guided by the *Standards for the English Language Arts* (1996) created by the International Reading Association (IRA) and the National Council of Teachers of English (NCTE). These standards serve to create consistency across all states with regard to the essential language arts skills and strategies that all students need to master to become literate adults. Consequently, because of the adoption of state standards and curricula based on the IRA/NCTE standards and the work of the National Reading Panel, educators nationwide have focused on the essential skills and strategies that children—beginning with the youngest students—will need in order to become productive literacy learners.

Furthermore, the No Child Left Behind (NCLB) legislation established by the U.S. federal government in 2001 requires all states to administer English language arts assessments in grades 3 through 8. Essentially, these tests evaluate the effectiveness of language arts curricula taught to students in these grades. According to NCLB guidelines, all students must be reading at grade level by the end of grade 3. Due to this legislation, primary-grade teachers must focus their instruction on meeting state standards as well as teaching the essential skills of language arts instruction. But in addition, they must maintain an awareness of the curriculum contents that students above the primary level will need in order to demonstrate mastery on state assessments

The assessments that have been established to measure both the effectiveness of state curricula and student mastery of essential skills and strategies have created concerns for everyone involved in educating children. Every school in every district across the United States must now take steps to ensure that all students, beginning in kindergarten, are taught the essential skills and strategies necessary for writing and reading success. Furthermore, teachers are concerned about how to create a balance in an already overloaded curriculum. Collectively, teachers, school administrators, and parents show a growing anxiety over how schools will continue to provide quality reading and writing instruction that addresses the state standards but is not overshadowed by the state-mandated assessments.

Teachers in grades 3 through 8 cannot effectively teach all the essential skills and strategies needed for students to achieve reading success on state-mandated assessments, and students cannot realistically learn all the essential skills and strategies needed to achieve success on state-mandated assessments within the few months preceding an examination (Guthrie, 2002). Consequently, teaching these essential skills—laying the foundation for successful literacy learning as well as achievement on the state-mandated assessments—must begin in kindergarten. For this reason, too, it seems necessary that schools establish a continuum of literacy learning in which students in grades K–3 study the same skill sets year after year, expanding their knowledge and skills in each area during each grade. This can ensure that students are not only prepared for state-mandated assessments but also prepared to be lifelong literacy learners. It is my hope that this book can get you started on that continuum.

Addressing the Challenge

The method and manner of how these skills are being taught has created even greater concerns. Several years ago, after the initial fourth-grade state-mandated assessment was introduced in New York state, elementary educators realized that this was actually a grade K–4 test because of the skills requirements assessed by the test. Our local Board of Cooperative Educational Services invited a group of primary-grade teachers to meet and design tasks for primary-grade students that would align with the tasks required of fourth-grade students on the New York state-mandated assessment. Although this was a commendable attempt to prepare our youngest students to meet the demands of the test, the result was workbooks containing test questions from the fourth-grade requirements adapted to a primary-grade level. There was little or no instruction providing the foundation necessary to learn the prerequisite language arts strategies necessary for mastery by grade 4. Would test preparation result in endless workbook-type tasks with no foundational instruction?

Many teachers who faced the challenge of preparing students in early grades for high-stakes, state-mandated assessments shared my concern. Recognizing that teachers needed to continue "best practices" teaching and learning in order for students to be successful on these assessments, I understood that a strong, basic, research-based literacy-skills model needed to be established in kindergarten through grade 3. Furthermore, this instruction had to translate into a continuous curriculum focused on essential literacy learning—one that would prepare students for state-mandated assessments while simultaneously supporting students in learning to read and respond with understanding, reading to gain information, learning how to select appropriate text, reading for enjoyment, and learning to write for a variety of purposes and audiences. In short, students need to be prepared for state-mandated assessments but, more importantly, need to learn how to become lifelong literacy learners.

Creating a Balanced Literacy Model

Several years prior to the federal government's mandates concerning standards and assessments, we decided at my elementary school to examine how to create a more comprehensive, cohesive language arts block across grade levels. Several teachers from various grade levels and I, the literacy specialist, met in study groups, and guided by the work of Fountas and Pinnell (1996, 2000, 2001), Calkins (1994, 2001), and Cunningham and Allington (1999) we decided to adopt a balanced literacy model for reading and writing instruction. We chose this model because

> A balanced reading approach is research-based, assessment-based, comprehensive, integrated, and dynamic in that it empowers teachers and specialists to respond to the individually assessed literacy needs of children as they relate to their appropriate instructional and developmental levels of decoding, vocabulary, reading comprehension, motivation, and sociocultural acquisition, with the purpose of learning to read for meaning, understanding, and joy. (Cowen, 2003, p. 10)

Our decision to proceed with a balanced literacy model was also supported by a number of professional texts, such as Pressley (1998) and Gentry (2000), and several important studies on reading approaches and strategy instruction, including *Becoming a Nation of Readers* (Anderson, Hiebert, Scott, & Wilkinson, 1985), *Preventing Reading Difficulties in Young Children* (National Research Council, 1998), and the *Report of the National Reading Panel* (NICHD, 2000). We also looked to the work of Palincsar and Brown (1984) on reciprocal teaching; Duffy and colleagues (1987) on the effect of explaining to students the reasoning for using reading strategies; Pressley, Johnson, Symons, McGoldrick, and Kurita (1989) and Duke and Pearson (2002) on strategies that improve children's comprehension; Anderson, Wilson, and Fielding (1988) on the importance of independent reading to raise reading achievement; and Raphael (1986) on Question–Answer Relationships. All this information established a strong research base for implementing a balanced literacy model based on workshop-style teaching that relies on teacher modeling, guided student practice, independent student practice, and assessment. One of the advantages of the balanced literacy model, too, is the immersion of students in a variety of authentic reading and writing experiences that support the basic concepts instrumental to successful standards mastery. (Table 1 shows the implementation and benefits of each component of the balanced literacy model.)

These understandings, such as the need for purposeful writing and information gathering, served as the minilessons modeled during a whole-group "writer's talk" (Fountas & Pinnell, 2001), then were reinforced during shared and small-group guided writing, and finally were assessed during independent writing sessions by conferring with students about the contents of their writing pieces, journals, or writer's notebooks.

Similarly, in the reading portion of the curriculum, read-aloud sessions allowed for the modeling of essential reading skills; shared reading provided practice of skills in a risk-free, interactive, whole-group context; guided reading sessions supported small-group, scaffolded instruction; and independent reading presented individual practice time and teacher–student conferring sessions (Blanton & Wood, 1984).

Furthermore, the structures inherent in teaching writing and reading within a balanced literacy model permitted the essential skills to be adjusted to meet individual variations in student achievement. For example, when working with a student or a group of students at various levels, the instructional focus concerning an essential skill could have remained constant, but the tools used for the instruction could have been varied by using different text levels for guided reading and independent reading or by choosing alternate texts for modeling and thinking aloud during whole-group minilessons.

Putting the Balanced Literacy Model Into Action

In addition to the guidelines mentioned above, the balanced literacy model we established focused on explicit strategy instruction and a gradual release of responsibility for the learning shifting from teacher to student (Pearson & Gallagher, 1983). These objectives were supported by workshop-style teaching, and they included time for guided and independent practice.

To support the phonics, phonemic awareness, and word study portion of the curriculum, we relied heavily on using effective approaches from

Table 1. Implementation and Benefits of a Balanced Literacy Model

Component	Implementation	Benefits
Read-Aloud	Teachers model strategies to the whole class by reading texts selected from various genres.	Allows teachers to demonstrate the application of essential reading and writing strategies Allows teachers to model what good reading sounds like Allows teachers access to a wide variety of genres at different levels of text difficulty
Shared Reading	Teachers initially read text to the whole class, pointing out essential skills and vocabulary. Both teachers and students share the reading of the text, generally multiple times over several days.	Allows teachers to introduce and model essential skills in a meaningful context Allows for risk-free reading practice
Guided Reading	Teachers form small, homogeneous groups based on similar needs and abilities. Teachers use leveled text correlated to students' reading abilities. Teachers guide the reading as the students practice.	Allows for flexible grouping and changes based on assessment Allows for additional practice with teacher guidance
Independent Reading	Students choose text and apply reading strategies while reading independently at appropriate levels. Teachers confer with students to assess student's abilities and monitor their reading levels.	Allows students a direct application of instruction in an authentic reading situation
Interactive Writing	Teachers and students compose a story together and then "share the pen" (take turns writing parts of the story).	Provides opportunities for students to practice essential skills such as concepts of print, letter–sound correspondence, spelling, and punctuation
Shared Writing	Teachers and students compose messages and stories together. Teachers model the writing.	Provides opportunities for teachers to model what good writers do Allows teachers and students to plan, compose, revise, and edit together
Guided Writing	Teachers instruct during a minilesson or conference and then guide the writing of a small group of students.	Allows teachers to introduce new skills or reinforce previously taught skills
Independent Writing	Students write independently. Teachers assist students by guiding and assessing the writing during individual conferences.	Allows students to practice writing Allows teachers to assess student writing
Word Work	Teachers instruct either the whole class or small groups in phonemic awareness, phonics, spelling, high-frequency words, or vocabulary.	Allows students instruction in decoding and vocabulary necessary to gain access to the reading process

Cunningham and her colleagues (Cunningham, 2000; Cunningham & Hall, 1998), as well as those from Fountas and Pinnell (1998). Multiple copies of texts housed in our reading closet were leveled based on the system created by Fountas and Pinnell (1999), who also provided us with a clear vision of how to structure small-group guided reading sessions using these leveled text sets (see Fountas & Pinnell, 1996, 2000). All classroom libraries throughout our building were also leveled (Fountas & Pinnell, 1999, 2001). This was essential in order to facilitate daily independent reading sessions that were structured according to the work of Taberski (2000). Finally, Keene and Zimmermann (1997), Harvey and Goudvis (2000), and Miller (2002) supplied the comprehension strategies on which we focused, as well as the instructional techniques of reading aloud from quality children's literature to teach comprehension strategies.

The foundation was laid for implementing writers' workshops in primary-grade classrooms by (a) enabling teachers to attend summer reading and writing institutes at Teachers College, Columbia University; (b) utilizing professional development resources in our building; and (c) forming study groups around the work of Fletcher (1996, 1999, 2000), Heard (1999) Ray (2001), and other noted authors in the field of teaching writing to children.

In making these decisions we realized that although other instructional frameworks exist with varying reading and writing components, it is most important to focus on the delivery of the reading and writing instruction within the model you choose. For example, while teacher modeling, scaffolding of student learning through guided instruction, independent practice, and assessment are at the heart of workshop-style teaching, these components can and should be incorporated into any instructional model. The requisite goal of all models should be guiding students toward strategy and skill acquisition, which will allow them to lead productive, literate lives.

Establishing Essential Skills in Writing and Reading

Effective instructional strategies were established at my school before the state-mandated assessments became an issue. When the assessments were introduced, the task of preparing students starting at the kindergarten level for future high-stakes tests became one of quality control. While we wanted to prevent the primary-grade language arts curriculum from turning into a test preparation curriculum, it was clear we needed to build in essential skill and strategy instruction necessary for future success on state-mandated assessments.

Examining state standards and research done by the New Standards Primary Literacy Committee (1999) and the *Learning Standards for English Language Arts* (New York State Department of Education, 1996) helped identify common threads in the construction of state standards, curricula, and assessments. I identified the essential skills from review of the above mentioned resources and from examination of the state standards and English language arts assessments in Arkansas, California, Connecticut, Florida, Georgia, Massachusetts, New Jersey, New York, North Carolina, and Texas. This sample of states was chosen because they represented both large and small states and covered several geographic locations. I found the following to be essential writing skills for primary-grade students:

- Students understand that writing has different purposes and those differences dictate the form the writing will take.
- Students are able to communicate their thoughts and feelings, and they can give and get information through written communication.
- Students can tell stories in written form from their own lives and the lives of others.

I found the following to be essential skills in reading and written response to reading for primary-grade students:

- Students understand that a story has a structure that allows it to make sense.
- Students understand that a story is built around certain elements—character, setting, problem, and solution. These elements allow a story to make sense.
- Students are able to recognize that stories and characters change over time and that precipitous events in the story mark the change.
- Students are able to recognize that a story has a main idea, and they are able to support this recognition with details from the story in verbal or written form.
- Students are able to answer a question or validate a theory or opinion in verbal or written form by reading and comparing and contrasting two or more pieces of text with supporting details.
- Students need to be able to read from a wide variety of genres and recognize the characteristics of various genres in order to aid in their own writing and understanding of text.

Creating Writing and Reading Continua

In the section of the report by the National Reading Panel that introduces the scientific evidence regarding reading comprehension instruction, Durkin (cited in

NICHD, 2000) states that comprehension has come to be viewed as "the essence of reading" (p. 4-39). The report further states that comprehension instruction should begin as early as kindergarten and that a solid, developmentally appropriate continuum of instruction is necessary for students to master essential reading and writing skills. After reviewing the IRA/NCTE standards (1996), the work of the New Standards Primary Literacy Committee (1999), and the joint position statement of IRA and the National Association for the Education of Young Children (NAEYC;1998), it was apparent that in order to help primary-grade teachers begin to incorporate these standards and assessments into their teaching methods, it was necessary to create a continuum of essential skills. It was necessary that the continuum should (a) focus on writing, reading, and response to reading skills and strategies; (b) begin in kindergarten, then move through grade 3; and (c) be embedded in a balanced literacy model. Also, developing this continuum would lead to a cyclical teaching approach, whereby skills are introduced, reintroduced, and expanded upon at subsequent grade levels. This cyclical approach would offer regular education students, special education students, English-language learners, and struggling learners more opportunity for mastery.

The continua of writing and reading outcomes presented in Tables 2 and 3 represent the basic skills that children must master to meet state standards as they progress through the primary grades. Acquisition of the essential skills outlined in the continua will allow students to become strong literacy learners and will provide them with background knowledge necessary to perform well on state-mandated assessments. These skills, such as writing a story within a narrative structure or recognizing the characteristics of a genre, are included in all state standards documents and state-mandated assessments.

Reading and writing are developmental processes in which learners go through predictable stages of development (IRA & NAEYC, 1998). As students move from grade level to grade level, the essential skills build on what was previously learned to create a seamless developmental skills curriculum, which moves students toward the goal of becoming members of the literacy community as well as being able to meet the demands of state-mandated assessments.

Filling in the Details: Units of Study in Writing and Reading

Beyond the development of the continua, the specific content of each lesson at each grade level had to be developed, and this was driven by discussions with teachers about how the essential skills should look at the various levels. The teachers also wanted to maintain consistency around the structure of the lessons, the literacy routines, and the language used for instruction. In other words, the learning would be more comfortable and powerful for students if they were ta-

Table 2. Continuum of Outcomes in Writing, Grades K–3

Unit of Study	Grade Level	Outcomes
Functional Writing	K	Students will recognize, understand, and become familiar with the different forms writing takes.
	1	Students will understand that we write in different ways for different purposes.
	2	Students will understand that different types of writing have different structures.
	3	Students will understand that the purpose of the writing drives the structure.
Letter Writing	K	Students will recognize and become familiar with the structure of a friendly letter (opening, body, closing).
	1	Students will understand purposes of writing a friendly letter.
	2	Students will understand purposes for writing a friendly letter, as well as the characteristics of what may be included.
	3	Students will become familiar with the purpose of each component in the structure of a friendly letter and understand that there is variety within each component.
Personal Narrative	K	Students will recognize and understand that a personal narrative is a story from or about one's own life.
	1	Students will understand that a personal narrative has a structure.
	2	Students will understand that in addition to structure, a personal narrative has a specific focus.
	3	Students will understand that a personal narrative has a focus, a structure, and details to enhance understanding and interest.

miliar with these elements and did not have to relearn classroom routines and instructional language from year to year. Teachers also felt it created more consistency for them if they knew how the learning was delivered in the grade levels before and after their own. Consequently, to meet all of these needs the format of the lesson plans for both the writing and reading units of study had to remain constant from grade level to grade level.

In the resulting curriculum, all the units adhere to a workshop-style method of teaching. The writing units begin with an immersion, which is the introductory phase of the unit. During this phase students receive explicit instruction around the writing objective they will be learning. The teacher models the writing or uses trade books that demonstrate the type of writing the students will focus on during the unit. Next, during the collecting phase, students try out various ideas and experiment with their own writing. After several days

Table 3. Continuum of Outcomes in Reading and Written Response to Reading, Grades K–3

Unit of Study	Grade Level	Outcomes
Story Structure	K	Students will understand that a story has a beginning, a middle, and an end and that this structure allows the story to make sense.
	1	Students will understand that a story has a beginning, a middle, and an end, and they can demonstrate this knowledge by retelling a story in proper sequence.
	2	Students will understand that a story has a structure, main idea, and supporting details, and students will understand how to use a graphic organizer to represent these story elements
	3	Students will understand that using a graphic organizer to sequence a text according to its structure (emphasizing the main idea and supporting details in each section) will help to construct a written response to reading that will make sense.
Story Elements	K	Students will understand that a story is centered on important parts that allow it to make sense.
	1	Students will be able to verbally define a story's elements and explain how they allow the story to make sense.
	2	Students will understand how to use these elements to retell a story both verbally and in written form.
	3	Students will understand how to formulate an extended written response using story elements to construct meaning.
Change Over Time	K	Students will understand that characters can change from the beginning to the end of a text and that precipitous events in the text can cause or support the change.
	1	Students will be able to recognize the events that cause a character's feeling or behaviors to change.
	2	Students will recognize these events and be able to find evidence to support the change.
	3	Students can support in written form (both graphic organizer and narrative) character changes from within a story or across a series.
Characteristics of Genre	K	Students will understand that text can be fiction, nonfiction, or poetry.
	1	Students will understand that within each genre there are different categories—for instance, fictional text can be folk tale, mystery, etc.
	2	Students will understand that each genre has it own characteristics and language.
	3	Students will read different genres and use prior experience (schema) to recognize, predict, and comprehend the differences between genres.

(continued)

Table 3. Continuum of Outcomes in Reading and Written Response to Reading, Grades K–3 (continued)

Unit of Study	Grade Level	Outcomes
Recognizing the Main Idea	K	Students will understand that a text has a main idea. The main idea is what the text is mostly about.
	1	Students will understand that a text has a main idea and supporting details that connect to the main idea.
	2	Students will be able to retell a text around the main idea and the supporting details.
	3	Students will be able to support the main idea with details both orally and in written form.
Compare/Contrast/ Conclude	K	Students will understand that similarities and differences occur between texts and that we draw conclusions about text based on these similarities and differences.
	1	Students will understand that opinions are formed and supported by the similarities and differences between texts.
	2	Students will be able to use a graphic organizer to support an opinion based on evidence found in different texts.
	3	Students will be able to support an opinion in written form using the similarities or differences found between texts.

of experimenting students will choose an idea to develop, then draft a finished product. Finally, students will practice revising, which involves making decisions about their writing, and then editing for correctness. During these phases students are guided by the teacher throughout the learning. (These stages are detailed in Table 4.)

The reading and response to reading units begin with the teacher modeling the use of a reading strategy. This minilesson is done during a whole-class session. The teacher generally reads a book, stopping to think aloud, explaining how the specific reading strategy being introduced will be used. Students get to practice the strategies during guided reading, which generally takes place in a small group led by the teacher using a leveled text. Students also independently practice the strategies by reading "just-right" books, which are self-selected text appropriate to their individual reading levels. (These stages are detailed in Table 5.) Variations from this outlined model may occur because certain steps may not be appropriate at a particular grade level.

Assessment of student learning weaves its way throughout all phases of all the units. Most assessment is done by conferring with individuals or small groups of students while they are writing or reading. In addition, teachers at

Table 4. Unit of Study Format—Writing

Phases	What Happens
Immersion	Students are introduced to the writing unit through minilessons, shared discussions, read-alouds, inquiry, and investigations.
Collecting	Students experiment with their writing by collecting and trying out different ideas.
Choosing and Developing an Idea	Students decide on an idea to develop and then practice and experiment with their writing.
Drafting	Students work toward creating a finished product.
Revising	Students make decisions about the content of their writing.
Editing	Students check and correct the mechanics of their writing.

Table 5. Unit of Study Format—Reading and Written Response to Reading

Phases	What Happens
Modeling	Students are introduced to the reading units through minilessons, shared reading, read-alouds, and think-alouds.
Guided Reading	Students take part in large-group, small-group, or partner sharing of text, charting of ideas, and trying out new learning.
Independent Reading	Students practice the new learning while reading and responding independently.
Follow-Up Activities	Students are given suggestions for future activities to keep the learning alive and relevant.

any time may assess a student's writing by checking a notebook or writing folder for mastery of an essential skill or by comparing the student's work over time to note progress. At different times during both guided and independent reading, teachers can do a running record or ask students to complete various reading response forms. Teachers assess a student's reading-response notebook for evidence of strategy learning. Reading logs also provide windows into progress by showing that a student is reading across genres or moving up levels. If after using some of these recommended assessments it is determined that some students have not mastered the essential skill addressed in the unit, the lessons can be reintroduced using different texts as resources (see Table 6).

Table 6. Assessments for Reading and Writing

Assessment Tools for Writing	Assessment Tools for Reading	Teacher Assesses to
Observation	Observation	Determine mastery of strategies and skills
Individual or small-group conferences	Running records	Determine reading levels
Rubrics	Individual Reading Inventories	Inform instruction
Writing journals, notebooks, or folders	Retelling	Reflect on the teaching
Student surveys	Written responses to reading, including reading response sheets, reading logs, journals, or notebooks	Form flexible groups for instruction
	Individual or small-group conferences	
	Reading assessment inventories, including running records	
	Student surveys	

Beyond State-Mandated Assessments: How to Use This Book in Your Classroom

To help you put this model into practice in your own classroom, all units of study presented in this book are ordered by grade level. The essential skills that students are expected to master at the appropriate grade levels are included, as are the materials and suggested texts necessary to effectively teach the lesson. Each segment of the numbered procedure list in a unit of study indicates a new minilesson that can be introduced on a subsequent day. You should determine the length of time required for each minilesson based on knowledge of your own classroom and students' abilities. Most of the essential skills in each of the units should be reintroduced and reinforced throughout the year.

Follow-up activities can be used in the days directly following the initial introduction of a lesson to extend learning, or they can be introduced at a later point during the year to reinforce a previously taught skill. The number of activities you choose to do should be decided by assessing how well your students have mastered an essential skill. Each of the follow-up activities should be introduced with a minilesson during a whole-group session.

The IRA/NCTE *Standards for the English Language Arts* (1996) provide ample possibilities for innovative, creative teaching vital to the learning process that enables students to become successful writers and readers. The goal of this book is to provide primary-grade teachers with an instructional tool that can help prepare students to master essential skills at their grade level, at higher grade levels, and ultimately on standards-based, state-mandated assessments. It is not necessary to teach the units in order; teachers can choose a unit and decide where and when it will fit best in the existing curriculum that they follow. Ideally, these continua or similar ones should be adopted across and between grade levels throughout a school or a district. If an individual teacher, however, decides to go it alone, the lessons are still beneficial outside the continua because of the skill sets they help build. In reality, mastery of the essential skills presented in this book goes beyond preparation for state-mandated assessments. After all, these are the skills students need to master in order to be prepared to lead productive, literate lives.

CHAPTER 2

Kindergarten: Introducing Essential Skills

Kindergarten is a time of wonder and excitement for young learners, mainly because for many students this is their first school experience, and formal learning is fresh and new for them. However, if teachers have responsibility for moving kindergartners toward mastery of essential skills required by state standards and achieving success on state-mandated assessments, the question is "How do these essential skills lessons look at the kindergarten level?"

The balanced literacy model and essential literacy skills outlined in chapter 1 will be introduced in kindergarten. Then, following a cyclical approach to teaching and learning, these same skills will be reintroduced and expanded upon in grades 1, 2, and 3, because these skills serve as the backbone of literacy learning and mastery of these skills is required by state learning standards and state-mandated assessments.

In these units, kindergarten students will learn to make decisions about what form to choose (either in writing, pictorially, or orally) in order to give or get information from their writing. They will create invitations and thank-you cards. They will learn how to label important items and create lists to keep track of important information. They will tell stories from their own lives when they write personal narratives, and they will learn how to write letters in order to give and get information. They will learn that because different types of writing take on different forms, they will need to write in different ways for different purposes. To help them with this learning, the writing units of study will focus on the following concepts and skills: functional writing (writing that informs), letter writing (writing that goes out into the world), and personal narrative (stories from personal life written in a narrative structure).

Each of the minilessons during the immersion stage of the units should take approximately 10–15 minutes. Drafting should also take about 15 minutes during the early studies but can expand to about 20 minutes later in the school year. The time allowed for revising and editing will depend on the needs of your classroom, but on average 10–15 minutes for revising and 10–15 minutes for editing should be sufficient in each unit.

The reading lessons introduce kindergarten students to the notion that reading is more than recognizing words on a page. They will learn that the essence of reading is making meaning. The reading units of study will focus on how a story's structure and its elements help it to make sense; how to recognize the characteristics of various genres in order to increase comprehension when reading in that genre; how to compare, contrast, and draw conclusions about text; how to recognize character or story changes that open a window into key plot development; and how to recognize the main idea of a text in order to increase comprehension.

Although many kindergarten students may not be actually reading text, they can and should be included in all the sessions outlined in the units of study. These experiences will move students toward becoming members of the literacy community. For example guided reading practice in kindergarten can be replaced by guided experience for students who are not yet ready to access print but can gain other literacy strategies and skills by sharing and discussing a common text in a small group. For example, during a guided experience with scaffolding from the teacher, kindergartners can look at a common text and then practice retelling stories using the picture clues, they can learn to clarify comprehension by asking questions, and they can learn to critique text by pointing to evidence from the story to back up an opinion. Likewise, during an independent experience, students can learn to independently choose a text at an appropriate level, examine the text, and then discuss the text with other members of the class.

At the kindergarten level the minilessons in the immersion stage of the reading units should take approximately 15 minutes. Earlier in the school year, guided reading should be about 10–15 minutes but should expand to 15–20 minutes later in the school year. Likewise, independent reading should be about 10–15 minutes expanding to about 15–20 minutes later in the year.

The lessons that follow should help kindergarten teachers establish the literacy learning foundation necessary to help students reach mastery of essential skills in later grades.

Kindergarten Writing Units

Functional Writing

Essential Skill

Students will recognize, understand, and become familiar with some of the different forms functional writing—or writing from which a reader gets practical information—can take.

Materials

- Samples of functional writing, such as invitations, business cards, thank-you notes
- Chart paper with Writing That We Get Information From written at top
- Assorted blank paper, blank notecards, and list paper (see Appendix A)
- Books centered on functional writing (see Suggested Texts)
- Kindergarten High-Frequency Word List (see Appendix B)

Procedure

Immersion

1. Bring in some samples of functional writing—invitations, menus, recipes, business cards, advertisements, posters, certificates, shopping lists, cereal boxes, clothing labels, food labels, driving directions, and so on—to show to the students.

2. Ask students to bring in samples of functional writing from home that they either wrote or received.

3. Share the samples and then place them in baskets according to various categories, such as Invitations, Directions, etc. Place the baskets in a writing center or on a table for viewing.

4. Read books during minilessons that highlight functional writing (see Suggested Texts).

Collecting

5. Ask students to explore the classroom looking for functional writing.

6. Follow up with a school walk pointing out functional writing or environmental print, such as exit signs and lavatory door labels, in the school building. (Leave one area of the building unexplored, and as a follow-up activity on another day have students act as print detectives, exploring and then sharing the print they find.)

7. Create a chart titled Writing That We Get Information From and ask students to paste their examples on the chart. Students can label the type of writing themselves or ask for assistance.

8. After completing the chart, discuss the information gathered from each type of writing and discuss why each type of writing is important.

9. Place various types of paper, blank notecards, blank postcards, and so forth in the writing center and allow students to experiment making posters and writing lists, notes, and invitations.

Choosing and Developing an Idea

10. As a whole class create an occasion such as a Celebrity Reader Day. Before writing an invitation to a celebrity reader such as the principal or school nurse, brainstorm with students about the type of information that should be included in the invitation.

Drafting

11. On chart paper, interactively write an invitation to the principal or another staff member, asking him or her to read to the class. This interactive experience is a whole-group shared writing experience—the students help compose the text; then they "share the pen," which means you write some of the text; then with help from you and other students several volunteers write some of the text. The goals are to practice using sound–symbol correspondence when writing words, to reinforce knowledge of high-frequency words, and to increase competency in the use of punctuation and capitalization.

Revising

12. During minilessons select certain samples and explain that in order for the reader to learn from these types of functional writing, specific information must be included. For example, show an invitation and explain that it must include the date, time, and location of the event in order for the reader to get all of the necessary information.

13. Have students select a piece of their own writing from when they were collecting pieces or experimenting in the writing center, then add important information that they think is missing.

Editing

14. Interactively write a thank-you note to one of the celebrity readers. "Share the pen" with students, stressing the use of capital letters at the beginning of each sentence.

15. Introduce the use of a period at the end of a sentence.

Follow-Up Activities

• During a whole-class minilesson, explain that paper and writing implements will be placed in each of the classroom learning centers. Explain that this is happening because writing is an important part of all we do and doesn't just happen

Figure 1. Friendly Letter Chart

People to Write To	Reason for Writing
Principal	Invite her to read to us
Custodian	Fix our shelf

Figure 2. Student Correspondence Chart

Student Name	Whom I Am Writing To	Reason for Writing
Kyle	Amy	Invite her to a party
Zachary	Grandma	Invite her to come and visit

Drafting

7. **Shared**—Together with students select a recipient for a class letter from the two-column chart generated previously. Discuss the three major components of a friendly letter (opening, body, closing). Also discuss how these components help the letter make sense. Then interactively draft the letter.

8. **Guided**—Give each student a sample friendly letter (see Appendix A) to read, and give them each three different colored sticky notes. Assign each color to indicate a component of the letter (for instance, pink = opening, green = body, yellow = closing), and ask students to attach the sticky notes to the appropriate components in the sample friendly letter.

9. **Independent**—Ask students to write a friendly letter to the person they named when generating the three-column chart. Make sure students know why they are writing the letter and that they include the three major components of a friendly letter.

Revising

10. Have students reread their letters and either add more information or remove unnecessary information.

11. Ask students to read their letters to a partner. Have the partners use the color-coded sticky notes to check for the three major components of the letter.

Editing

12. Post high-frequency words on a word wall (see Appendix B). Ask students to check their letters to see if familiar high-frequency words are spelled correctly.

Follow-Up Activities

• Create a chart-size, color-coded letter in the writing center labeled with the three major parts of a friendly letter. Have students continue to independently write letters to outside recipients or to one another when they visit the class-room writing center

- Continue to interactively write letters with oral input from students.
- Ask parents, grandparents, or other relatives to become pen pals with the students, providing them with authentic opportunities to write.

Assessment

Students will demonstrate the ability to recognize the parts of a friendly letter. At the conclusion of the introductory letter-writing unit, schedule individual conferences with each student during learning center time.

- Have a sample letter available. Read the letter, then ask the student to point out specific parts of the letter. Check for the student's understanding that these parts are necessary because they help the letter make sense.
- If students have written their own letters, have them read the letter and point out the three components. Kindergarten students may elect to draw the entire contents of their letters or add a few words and orally retell it. This is acceptable at this level.

Suggested Texts

Ahlberg, J., & Ahlberg, A. (2001). *The jolly postman or other people's letters*. Boston: Little, Brown.

Campbell, R. (1982). *Dear zoo*. New York: Four Winds Press.

Caseley, J. (1991). *Dear Annie*. New York: Greenwillow.

James, S. (1996). *Dear Mr. Blueberry*. New York: Simon & Schuster.

Keats, E.J. (1998). *A letter to Amy*. New York: Penguin.

Pak, S. (2001). *Dear Juno*. New York: Penguin.

Personal Narrative

Essential Skill

Students will recognize that a personal narrative is a story from or about your own life.

Materials

- Writing Ideas sheet (one for each student; see Appendix A)
- Personal Narrative Writing Rubric (see Appendix B)

Procedure

Immersion

1. Introduce the idea that authors use their own lives to get writing ideas. Follow up by introducing the term *personal narrative* and define it as a story from or about one's own life. Continue by telling an interesting story from your own life.

2. Read trade books with stories that may have come from an author's life (see Suggested Texts).

3. During the next several days have the students share personal stories in large or small groups.

4. The following week tell another personal story leaving out a lot of details. Discuss with the class how to make the story more interesting. Introduce the term *details* and define it as the pieces of information we add to a story to make it more interesting.

Collecting

5. Along with students, develop a list of topics that would make good stories (such as trips, parties, holiday gatherings, and playing with friends).

6. Using the Writing Ideas sheet, have the students write or draw one or two stories from their lives that they would like to share (see Appendix A). This can be done on different days using the same sheet or additional sheets.

Choosing and Developing an Idea

7. After using the Writing Ideas sheet several different times, have students look over their sheets to decide on an idea for a personal narrative.

8. Retell the personal story that you shared with the class previously, and model writing (drawing) it on paper. During a subsequent minilesson add words to the story.

Drafting

9. Have students use the idea they have chosen to write or draw a personal narrative.

Revising

10. Model how to add more details by inserting words into your story, enhancing your drawing, or labeling the pictures. Do this by retelling your original story and asking the students if there is other information missing from the original story that they are curious about. Select one or two suggested details to include in the story.

11. Ask the students to reread their personal narratives and add more detail; if they have drawn their stories, they can label the story with a few words.

12. Have students use the high-frequency word list to correct their stories.

Follow-Up Activities

- Have students make a cover for their personal narrative, making sure the cover matches the focus of their personal narrative. Refer to the covers of the texts used for this unit as examples. Point out how the cover reflects the focus of the story inside the book. Tell students that the cover of a book is generally designed after the story is completed.

- Have a publishing party to celebrate the completion of the personal narratives. Students can read their stories to one another or to invited guests.

- Repeat this series of lessons. However, during Revising, focus on eliminating unnecessary information from a piece of writing rather than adding information to a piece of writing.

- Create an ongoing chart of possible life events that could be used to write a personal narrative.

- Repeat this series of lessons focusing on adding words or sentences to a story.

Assessment

Students will demonstrate the ability to tell a personal narrative (orally or in written form) that is a based on a story from their own life.

- During the Editing and the Follow-Up phases of the study, take notes or use a rubric to see how well a student can stay focused and tell a personal narrative with relevant details (see Appendix B for the Personal Narrative Writing Rubric).

Suggested Texts

Carle, E. (1994). *My apron.* New York: Philomel Books.

Curtis, J.L. (1995). *When I was little: A four-year-old's memoir of her youth.* New York: HarperCollins.

Haskins, F. (1994). *Things I like about Grandma.* San Francisco: Children's Book Press.

Howard, A. (1999). *When I was five.* San Diego, CA: Harcourt.

Rockwell, A. (2004). *Welcome to kindergarten.* New York: Walker & Company.

Rockwell, A. (2005). *Apples and pumpkins.* New York: Simon & Schuster.

Tarpley, N.A. (2001). *I love my hair!* Boston: Little, Brown.

Kindergarten Reading and Response to Reading Units

Essential Skill

Students will understand that a story has a beginning, a middle, and an end and that this structure allows the story to make sense.

Materials

- Two familiar texts (recommended text *The Little Red Hen* [Barton, 1993] and the other is optional; see Suggested Texts)
- Retelling Rubric (see Appendix B)
- A large story web drawn on chart paper
- Three-column chart with column 1 labeled Beginning, column 2 labeled Middle, and column 3 labeled End

Procedure

Modeling

1. During a shared reading experience explain to the students that most stories have a beginning, a middle, and an end. Further explain that these parts make up the story's structure and that the structure holds the story together. The order of the parts (beginning, middle, and end) is important, because this order allows the story to make sense.

2. Follow the explanation of story structure by reading a familiar story, stopping to call attention to the beginning, middle, and end of the story. After reading say, "I wonder what would happen if I read the middle of the story first." Proceed to read the middle and then say, "This story doesn't make sense. I have to read the beginning first, the middle next, and the end last—otherwise the story won't make sense."

3. The following day read another familiar story and create a story web, placing the title of the story in the center cell and labeling the other three cells Beginning, Middle, and End. Then say, "We can't put all the information from each part of the story into the cells, so we need to think about the most important parts of the story to put in the cells." Retell each section of the story out loud, choosing and summarizing the most important parts to write in the cells.

4. In small groups repeat creating story webs for other stories, encouraging the students to retell and then summarize the information necessary to complete each cell. Ask several group members to retell the story to the whole group, or have the partners retell the story to each other.

5. Read a new story to the class. Follow up the reading by drawing a three-column chart. Use the title of the story for the heading at the top of the chart, and label column 1 Beginning, column 2 Middle, and column 3 End. Ask students to draw what happened in each section of the story (do one section per day). Paste their illustrations in the corresponding columns on the chart.

6. Place students in small groups and repeat this process again. Read a different story to each group. After the reading, place the students within the small groups into pairs. Assign a different section of the story to each of the pairs. Ask each group to retell their story to the class by having the pairs within the groups retell their part of the story.

Follow-Up Activities

• On a flannel board or chart create a complete story web for a familiar story (cell pieces must be movable). Place the cells in incorrect order. Read the web to the class and, with student help, reassemble the web in the correct order. Emphasize the idea that the structure must be sequenced correctly for the story to make sense.

• Write sections of a story on cards. Then read each section randomly to a small group. Together put the story in an order that makes sense. Then reread the story to the group.

• Interactively write the beginning, the middle, and the end of an original class story or a retelling of a familiar story.

Assessment

Students will demonstrate the ability to retell a story sequentially.

During learning center time or small group work, have students sequence stories on a flannel board and retell the story to the group.

• During the small-group retellings, take notes or use the Retelling Rubric (see Appendix B) to assess a student's retelling ability. Check for correct sequence of events and if the story makes sense.

Suggested Texts

Barton, B. (1993). *The little red hen.* New York: HarperCollins.

Hutchins, P. (1992). *You'll soon grow into them, Titch.* New York: Mulberry Books.

Krauss, R. (1945). *The carrot seed.* New York: HarperCollins.

Lionni, L. (1973). *Frederick.* New York: Random House.

Essential Skill

Students will understand that a story is centered on important parts that help it make sense.

Materials

• Several familiar texts (see Suggested Texts for suggestions)

• Three pieces of chart paper, individually labeled Character, Setting, and Events

• Drawing paper

Procedure

Modeling

1. Select a familiar story and say, "When authors think about a story they want to tell, they think about the structure of the story—what will happen in the beginning, the middle, and the end of the story. Then they think about other parts of the story that will help it make sense. If you compare a story to our body, the story structure is like our skeleton, which holds everything together, and the story elements are like our muscles, skin, eyes, hair, and all the things that make us unique."

2. Read a familiar story and then say, "This story had some people in it who helped to tell the story. These people are called the characters. Sometimes the characters are people, and sometimes they are animals or other things. Characters are important to help a story make sense."

3. Over subsequent days repeat this process using both familiar and new stories. Focus on introducing one story element (such as characters, setting, or events) with each story.

Guided Reading

4. Revisit the texts used to introduce story structure, such as *The Little Red Hen* (Barton, 1993). Label three different pages of chart paper with a story

element: Characters, Setting, Events. After reading the story ask students to identify the characters, then write the names of the characters on the chart. Have students select a character to illustrate and glue the illustrations on the chart. Repeat this process for each story element on a separate piece of chart paper. The charts should be hung up for future reference.

Independent Reading

5. Have the students choose a favorite book for independent reading. After students look at the book, distribute paper folded in two columns. Ask students to draw their favorite character from the story in column 1 and their favorite event in column 2. After the activity is complete have students share their sheets with a partner. Expand the number of story elements included on the sheet later in the year (for example, add settings).

Follow-Up Activities

• During small-group guided reading, read a variety of Big Books, trade books, and texts used for prior guided reading sessions. Model how to identify the story elements and use them as a guide for retelling the story, explaining how the elements help the listener to make sense of the story. Follow up by reading a new story, then have the students identify the story elements and retell the story focusing on the elements as a guide.

• During writing time, ask students to write or draw a story using paper folded in four boxes. Ask students to write or draw different events in each of the boxes. After the stories are complete, students can share their stories by introducing the characters, the setting, and the events as they happened in their stories. For example, a student would say, "The characters in my story are.... My story takes place in...and this is my story...." Ask the students to point to the events in each box as they tell the story.

• Choose a new familiar story. Create a chart divided in three columns. Label the columns Characters, Settings, and Events. On index cards write the character names, setting descriptions, and certain events from the story. Before reading the story aloud, read the cards and ask some students to place the cards in the correct columns. After reading, check to see if the cards were placed in the correct columns. (Figure 3 shows an example using the story of Little Red Riding Hood.)

Figure 3. Story Elements Chart

Characters	Settings	Events
Little Red Riding Hood	Forest	Little Red Riding Hood meets the wolf
Wolf	Grandma's house	The wolf tries to fool Little Red Riding Hood
Woodsman		Woodsman rescues Little Red Riding Hood

Assessment

The students will be able to retell and recognize the characters, the settings, and the events in a story.

• Use students' four-box stories and the oral retells to determine if the students can recognize and retell a story using the story elements.

• Repeat using the three-column chart and cards during small-group guided reading.

Suggested Texts

Barton, B. (1993). *The little red hen.* New York: HarperCollins.

Bottner, B. (1992). *Bootsie Barker bites.* New York: Penguin.

Cannon, J. (1993). *Stellaluna.* San Diego, CA: Harcourt.

Fox, M. (1990). *Shoes from Grandpa.* Danbury, CT: Orchard Books.

Henkes, K. (1996). *Chrysanthemum.* New York: Mulberry Books.

Krauss, R. (1945). *The carrot seed.* New York: HarperCollins.

Change Over Time

Essential Skills

Students will understand that a story and characters can change from the beginning to the end of the story and that precipitous events in the story can cause or support the change.

Materials

• Familiar Big Book
• Chart paper
• Drawing paper folded in half (one per student)

Procedure

Modeling

1. During shared reading time, read a familiar Big Book, such as *The Little Red Hen*, and revisit the web that was used to teach story structure. Retell the story using the web as a guide, calling specific attention to the beginning, the middle, and the end of the story. After the retell, say to the students, "I noticed while I was retelling the story that something else was happening that I needed to pay attention to. As the story went along, the Little Red Hen started to change how she acted. At first she thought her friends would help her make the bread and she was willing to share, but by the end of the story she realized they would not help so she decided to keep the bread for herself. I realized that many times a character's actions or feelings change from the beginning to the end."

2. The following day draw a timeline on chart paper marking the far-left point of the timeline with a Beginning and the far-right point of the timeline with an End. Write, under Beginning, "The Little Red Hen wanted to share." Then, under End, write "The Little Red Hen did not want to share." Ask the students what made her change. Write the causes as points on the timeline.

Guided Reading

3. In a small group, repeat the above lesson several times using familiar stories. Elicit character changes and precipitous events from the students.

4. Using multiple copies of the same text, read a story to the group. Then create a timeline eliciting from the group how a character acted at the beginning, and then how the character acted at the end, and what made the character change.

Independent Reading

5. In a small group after a read-aloud, give each student a paper folded in half. Label one half Beginning and the other half End. Ask the students to draw a picture of how the character acted at the beginning and then at the end. After the drawing discuss what made the character change.

Follow-Up Activities

• Repeat this process throughout the year with follow-up discussions and activities that focus on how a characters' feelings can change from the beginning to the end. For example, a character can start out sad and end up happy.

- Read familiar stories and ask the question "What lesson did the character learn at the end of this story?" Point out that many times when a character changes at the end of a story it is accompanied by learning a lesson. Good examples are stories such as *The Three Bears* (Galdone, 1986) or *The Three Billy Goats Gruff* (Galdone, 1981).

Assessment

The students will be able to recognize and explain the changes characters may experience during the course of a story.

- Using the drawings demonstrating character change, confer with students individually, asking them to explain why or how the character changed in the story.

Suggested Texts

Fox, M. (1989). *Koala Lou.* San Diego, CA: Harcourt.

Galdone, P. (1981). *The three billy goats Gruff.* New York: Clarion Books.

Galdone, P. (1986). *The three bears.* Boston: Houghton Mifflin.

Hutchins, P. (1992). *You'll soon grow into them, Titch.* New York: Mulberry Books.

Teague, M. (2004). *Pigsty.* New York: Scholastic.

Characteristics of Genre

Essential Skill

Students will understand that text can be fiction, nonfiction, or poetry.

Materials

- Basket of books from each genre—fiction, nonfiction, and poetry (see Suggested Texts)
- Chart paper

Procedure

Modeling

1. During a shared reading experience, gather together a basket of familiar books in various genres. Explain to students that there are many different types or categories of books and that sometimes we use the word *genre* to talk about a type of book. Hold up several fiction stories and say, "I was thinking that we have read a lot of stories like these. This genre or type of book is called fiction. Today I thought we would read another genre or type of book. This genre

is called nonfiction." Hold up a nonfiction book (such as *Chickens Aren't the Only Ones* [Heller, 1999]) and say, "After I read this book, I'm going to tell you what I was thinking about as I was reading." Read the book aloud and, when you're done reading, focus on some of the characteristics of nonfiction. For example, point out that the book is written to give us information about a topic rather than telling a story, the book has captions that contain information, and the book has detailed drawings that are labeled. Explain that because these types of books are different than the ones already displayed in the room, it would be a good idea to sort the books by their topics. After this discussion say, "I think it would be easier to find and choose books we like if we group some of our classroom books together and give them a category. The books that have stories the author made up are called fiction books, and the books that have real information about a topic are called nonfiction books."

Guided Reading

2. During a shared reading experience, create a chart with three columns and label two of the columns Fiction and Nonfiction; leave the last column blank. Over the course of several days read a few new books from the fiction and nonfiction genres, eliciting characteristics of each genre from the students. For example, nonfiction books usually contain many photographs and captions. With student input, place the books in baskets by genre, and decide on names for the categories created. Label the baskets with the names that students created for the categories. Students may label the baskets by classifying the books into different types of fiction and different topics in nonfiction; however the chart should contain broad characteristics of each genre.

3. Hold up a poetry book and say, "Now that we know a lot about fiction and nonfiction books, we need to learn about another genre or type of book: poetry. Books in this genre are different from fiction and nonfiction books, and as I read, you'll see how." Label the last column on the chart Poetry and, after you read the poetry book, elicit from the class several characteristics of poetry. (Figure 4 shows an example of the three-column characteristics of genre

Figure 4. Characteristics of Genre Chart

Fiction	Nonfiction	Poetry
Made-up stories	About real topics	Sometimes rhymes
Animals and objects can talk	Pictures and photographs	Words can be in different places on the page
	Captions	

chart.) For example, some characteristics of poetry include rhyme, rhythm, an unusual use of white space, and unique placement of words on the page.

4. Over the next few days, read several poems from different books and ask students to help you add characteristics of poetry to the chart.

Independent Reading

5. During independent reading, ask students to read or look at books from different genres. Make sure fiction, nonfiction, and poetry books are in the "just-right" books baskets. (Although "just-right" book baskets generally contain books at the students' individual reading levels, for this study it is fine to include some higher-level fiction, nonfiction, and poetry books for the students to review.) Familiar poems can be written on cards and included in the baskets as well.

Follow-Up Activities

• Create a class chart that lists and classifies titles read throughout the year during read-aloud and shared reading sessions.

• Give the students a book to look at and read with a partner. During shared reading time, the partners can tell the class what genre the book is and what characteristics helped them to recognize it as part of that genre.

• Throughout the year have the students continue to sort the classroom library by classifying books and creating baskets.

• Later in the year each student may keep a simple log that lists fiction, nonfiction, or poetry books they have read or examined independently.

• Create a fiction piece with input from the class. Review the need for the story to have a structure and contain story elements. On a subsequent day write a nonfiction piece with input from the class (for instance, instructions on caring for a pet). Ask students to create illustrations to accompany both pieces. Glue some of the illustrations on the story chart. On the nonfiction piece, label the drawings or create captions to go under the illustrations.

• Create a class Big Book containing favorite poems. As poems are added ask the students what they notice about each poem. Include these observations in the poetry column on the three-column genre characteristics chart. For example, write "This poem has a lot of space between each line" or "This poem has the words written in a circle."

• During writing workshop ask students to try out some of the techniques or characteristics of nonfiction or poetry in their own writing (introduce only one or two techniques at a time).

Assessment

Students will demonstrate an understanding of some of the unique characteristics of fiction, nonfiction, and poetry.

• After a read-aloud session, ask several students to identify the genre of the book. After they make a choice of genre type, ask them how they know it belongs to the genre they are choosing. Also ask them what it would have to contain if it were from a different genre.

• During writers' workshop conferences, ask the students what genre they are writing in, then ask them to point to or explain some of the genre's characteristics that they have included in their writing. Look for evidence of story structure, captions, creative use of white space, unique placement of words on the page, and so forth.

Suggested Texts

Nonfiction

Aliki. (1989). *My five senses*. New York: HarperCollins.

Asch, F. (2000). *The sun is my favorite star*. San Diego, CA: Harcourt.

Ehlert, L. (2000). *Waiting for wings*. San Diego, CA: Harcourt.

Heller, R. (1999). *Chickens aren't the only ones*. New York: Penguin.

Marzollo, J. (1996). *I am water*. New York: Scholastic.

Onyefulu, I. (1997). *A is for Africa*. New York: Penguin.

Riley, L.C. (1999). *Elephants swim*. Boston: Houghton Mifflin.

Rockwell, A. (1982). *Boats*. New York: Puffin.

Fiction

Crews, D. (1998). *Night at the fair*. New York: Greenwillow.

Fox, M. (1989). *Koala Lou*. San Diego, CA: Harcourt.

Henkes, K. (1997). *Chester's way*. New York: Mulberry Books.

Rylant, C. (1996). *The bookshop dog*. New York: Scholastic.

Wiesner, D. (2001). *The three pigs*. New York: Clarion Books.

Poetry

Florian, D. (1998). *Beast feast*. San Diego, CA: Harcourt.

Prelutsky, J. (1984). *The new kid on the block*. New York: Greenwillow.

Stevenson, J. (2000). *Cornflake poems*. New York: Greenwillow.

Compare/Contrast/Conclude

Essential Skill

Students will understand that similarities and differences occur between texts and that we draw conclusions about text based on these similarities and differences.

Materials

- Several books with variations of the same story (for instance, two versions of *The Three Billy Goats Gruff*; see Suggested Texts)
- Chart paper for T-charts
- Drawing paper folded in four boxes (one sheet per student)

Procedure

Modeling

1. During shared reading time, read a familiar text such as *The Three Billy Goats Gruff* (Asbjornsen & Moe, 1991). After reading the text say, "I was thinking that this book reminds me of another book called *The Three Billy Goats Gruff*, but it was written by someone else. Let's read it and see if the story is the same." Read the second version of the story and say, "This book is almost the same as the first one, but this author made some changes. I'm going to write down the things that are the same and the things that are different in the two stories." Create a compare–contrast T-chart and write down the similarities and differences between the two books (see Figure 5). After completing the chart say, "I learned authors can reuse ideas when they write stories. I came to the conclusion that sometimes they keep things the same and sometimes they change a few things. I'm also thinking that when books or characters are familiar to us and we know most of the characters and most of what is going to happen, it helps us to understand the book better."

2. In the next two shared reading sessions, read two different versions of another familiar story and continue to compare, contrast, and draw a conclusion about the similarities or differences between the two texts.

Figure 5. Compare–Contrast T-Chart

The Three Billy Goats Gruff Story 1 retold by P.C. Asbjornsen and J.E. Moe (1991) Story 2 retold by J. Stevens (1990)	
Things That Were the Same	**Things That Were Different**
There were three goats and one troll.	In story 1 the goats didn't wear clothes.
The goats were hungry.	In story 2 the goats wore clothes.
The troll lived under the bridge.	
The goats had to cross the bridge to get to the grass.	
The goats tricked the troll.	
The big goat kicked the troll into the water.	
Conclusion: Authors can reuse the same story by making some changes to the characters.	

Guided Reading

3. Begin the session by reminding students that when they looked at the two versions of *The Three Billy Goats Gruff,* they were looking for similarities and differences between the two books. Also remind them that the class came to the conclusion that different authors can use the same storyline, but they can decide to keep or change some of the details or characters. Hold up two versions of *The Three Bears* (Galdone, 1986; Marshall, 1998), and explain to students that today, instead of comparing and contrasting the two books, you are going to look at how the authors presented the main character, Goldilocks, in the two books. After either reading or looking through the books, ask students what they think about Goldilocks's behavior in the two books. Then say, "I think Goldilocks was being very naughty when she went into the bears' house. I think we need to look back inside these two books and see what the two different authors did to show us that Goldilocks was naughty." Create an Evidence of Inquiry T-chart and at the top write "Goldilocks was Naughty." With student input, list the evidence from both of the books to prove Goldilocks was naughty (see Figure 6). After completing the chart, explain to the students that although two versions of the same story may have different elements, the major elements will remain the same in each.

Independent Reading

4. Distribute drawing paper, and ask students to fold it into four boxes. After reading two versions of the same story, ask students to draw pictures in the top two boxes of something that is the same in both stories. The following day review the stories and then ask students to draw something in the bottom two boxes that is different in the two stories. Share drawings during a whole-class meeting.

Figure 6. Goldilocks Evidence of Inquiry T-Chart

Goldilocks Was Naughty
Story 1 retold by P. Galdone (1996)
Story 2 retold by J. Marshall (1998)

Story 1	Story 2
Goldilocks went into the bears' house uninvited.	Goldilocks went in the bears' house uninvited.
Goldilocks ate the bears' porridge.	Goldilocks ate the bears' porridge.
Goldilocks broke baby bear's chair.	Goldilocks broke baby bear's chair
Goldilocks slept in baby bear's bed.	Goldilocks slept in baby bear's bed.
Goldilocks ran away and didn't say thank you.	Goldilocks ran away and didn't say thank you.

Figure 7. Mean Sisters Evidence of Inquiry T-Chart

How Were the Sisters Mean to Cinderella?
Story 1 retold by B. Karlin (2001)
Story 2 retold by F. Minters (1997)

Story 1	Story 2
The sisters made her do all the work.	They didn't let her watch television or play video games.
They made her sleep in the ashes.	Cinder-Elly couldn't go shopping.
They called her names.	Cinder-Elly had to mop.
They didn't let her go to the ball.	

Follow-Up Activities

- During large-group shared reading sessions or small-group guided reading sessions, read different versions of the same story or different stories with similar story lines, such as *The Enormous Potato* (Davis, 1997) and *The Enormous Turnip* (Holmes, 1998). Continue to use the compare and contrast T-chart to examine texts. Also, make sure to draw conclusions about the two texts, such as authors can retell the same story using different characters.

- Draw an evidence of inquiry T-chart and create a focus question that can be proved with examples from two versions of a text. Emphasize the importance of looking back in the book for evidence to answer the question. For example, using two versions of *Cinderella* a focus question can be "How were the sisters mean to Cinderella in each of the stories?" Then ask students to look back in both texts to find examples. Write the evidence on the T-chart. (See Figure 7.)

- Introduce a Venn diagram or a Y-chart to plot similarities and differences between texts (see Appendix A for a reproducible Venn diagram and a reproducible Y-chart).

- Rewrite a familiar story with class input, making minor character or plot changes.

Assessment

Students will recognize and discuss similarities and differences between texts and will return to the text for evidence of their thinking.

- During independent or small-group reading, read two similar stories on two separate days to the students. Ask students to discuss the similarities and differences between the texts. Write their responses on a chart, making sure each student responds. Take note of the appropriateness of the responses.

- Using the two similar stories you have chosen, fashion a set of questions relevant to either the story line or characters in the texts. Ask students for answers, then ask them to show you how they know their responses are correct. Check to see if students can find the appropriate places in the texts to back up their thinking. For example, ask "How did Cinderella get to the ball?" or "What happened to Cinderella when she left the ball?"

Suggested Texts

Asbjornsen, P.C., & Moe, J.E. (1991). *The three billy goats Gruff*. San Diego, CA: Harcourt.

Davis, A. (1998). *The enormous potato*. Toronto, ON: Kids Can Press.

Galdone, P. (1983). *The gingerbread boy*. Boston: Houghton Mifflin.

Galdone, P. (1986). *The three bears*. Boston: Houghton Mifflin.

Holmes, S. (1998). *The enormous turnip*. New York: Penguin.

Karlin, B. (1989). *Cinderella*. New York: Scholastic.

Marshall, J. (1998). *The three bears*. New York: Penguin.

Minters, F. (1997). *Cinder-Elly*. New York: Penguin.

Stevens, J. (1990). *The three billy goats Gruff*. San Diego, CA: Harcourt.

Ziefert, H. (1995). *The gingerbread boy*. New York: Viking Press.

Main Idea

Essential Skill

Students will understand that a story has a main idea. The main idea is what the story is mostly about.

Materials

- *The Carrot Seed* (Krauss, 1945)
- Two-column chart with column 1 labeled Title and column 2 labeled Main Idea

Procedure

Modeling

1. During a shared reading session before reading a new book, introduce the book by saying, "Today we are going to read *The Carrot Seed*. This book is about a little boy who wants to grow carrots, but no one thinks he can do it." Read the book aloud. Then say, "When I introduced the book to you and told you what it was about, I was sharing the main idea. That is the idea I thought the author had when he decided to write this story. The main idea is what the

story is mostly about. Usually before someone writes a story they think about what the book is going to be about. Then, as they write, they add details to help us figure out the main idea. We need to pay attention to the details and we need to know most of the story before we can recognize the main idea."

2. After sharing information about main idea, create a two-column chart and write down several familiar book titles (see Figure 8). Next to each title, write the book's main idea. Then suggest that the students think about stories they know to add to the chart.

3. Reread a familiar text pointing out how the title, the opening thought, and the closing thoughts are details that an author uses to help us recognize the main idea. Emphasize how we need to pay attention to the title because the author chose it to help us know what the book will be about. We need to pay attention to the opening thoughts because usually something that is placed first is put there because it is important. We need to pay attention to the closing thoughts because those ideas are what the author left with us to re-member the book.

Guided Reading

4. Ask the class for titles that have been read during the year. Then ask what the main idea of each story is. Add these titles to the two-column chart you started in the Modeling session.

5. During small-group guided and shared reading, continue introducing new books by saying, "The story we are going to read is about.... This is the story's main idea."

6. After completing a guided reading book elicit the main idea of the book from the students. If a student is unsure, reword the question to ask what the book is mostly about.

Figure 8. Main Idea Chart

Title	Main Idea
Corduroy (Freeman, 1968)	This story is about a bear who lives in a toy shop for a long time and wishes he had friends and a home.
Brown Bear, Brown Bear, What Do You See? (Martin & Carle, 1992)	This story describes things that different animals and children see.
The Very Hungry Caterpillar (Carle, 1986)	This story describes the many things a caterpillar has to do before it turns into a butterfly.
Chicka Chicka Boom Boom (Martin & Archambault, 1992)	It is about some tricky alphabet letters.

7. After looking at a self-selected text ask students to draw the story's main idea. Pair students with partners and have them retell the story around the main idea, using the drawing as a guide.

Follow-Up Activities

- Introduce the connection between the main idea and supporting details and how adding a few important details can help when retelling a story around the main idea. Model how to retell a read-aloud by first saying, "The main idea in this story is...and some of the important things that happened in the story are...."

- Ask students to organize several book baskets, using similar main idea as the criterion for placement in a basket

- Use a story web to graphically represent the main idea and supporting details.

Assessment

Students will be able to use supporting details to identify the main idea of a text.

- Using the drawings previously done after a read-aloud, confer with the students individually and ask them to share their drawings and explain the story's main idea and supporting details.

Suggested Texts

Carle, E. (1986). *The very hungry caterpillar.* New York: Philomel Books.

Fox, M. (1991). *Possum magic.* San Diego, CA: Harcourt.

Freeman, D. (1968). *Corduroy.* New York: Viking Press.

Gordon, S. (1989). *Mike's first haircut.* New York: Troll.

Henkes, K. (1996). *Sheila Rae, the brave.* New York: Mulberry Books.

Hutchins, P. (1992). *You'll soon grow into them, Titch.* New York: Mulberry Books.

Krauss, R. (1945). *The carrot seed.* New York: HarperCollins.

Martin, B., Jr, & Archambault, J. (1992). *Chicka chicka boom boom.* New York: Simon & Schuster.

Martin, B., Jr, & Carle, E. (1992). *Brown bear, brown bear, what do you see?* New York: Holt, Rinehart and Winston.

CHAPTER 3

Grade 1: Continuing the Learning

Grade 1 is a year packed with new learning. It is the year when each student sitting in the classroom is expected to become a member of the literacy community. Learning to read and write are the goals for each child, and the teacher is expected to help each child realize those goals. Adding to these expectations are the concerns of administrators, other teachers, and parents that these grade 1 students develop into competent readers and writers who are prepared to meet the tasks required by state standards and assessments.

Although not all kindergartners are reading and writing as they move into grade 1, it becomes easier for students to master the essential skills if both a balanced literacy model of instruction and a cyclical, seamless curriculum are in place. Students immersed in these structures will be prepared to construct new meaning based on previous knowledge introduced in kindergarten. For instance, students who participated in writers' workshop in kindergarten should be able to generate ideas for their writing and be familiar with the steps in the writing process.

Writing in grade 1 is all about purpose; students will learn to ask themselves the question, What am I trying to communicate as a writer and how best can I do that? They will practice this by writing notes, invitations, posters, friendly letters, and personal narratives about important moments in their lives.

Students will use their kindergarten reading experiences and their knowledge of story structure and story elements to retell a story in a structured format centering on the main idea. They will learn to recognize that characters change in a story, and they will be able to explain some of the reasons for that change. Grade 1 students who have been and are being read to extensively will learn to point out the characteristics in different genres as well as recognize the similarities and differences between genres.

The suggested minilessons that are part of the first-grade writing units should take approximately 15 minutes each. Sessions that involve actual writing, such as when students choose, develop, and draft their ideas, should begin as 15-minute sessions but should extend to around 25–30 minutes later in the year; revising and editing should also start at about 15 minutes each, then later in the year extend to 25–30 minutes each.

The whole-class minilessons that are part of the reading units should take approximately 15 minutes. Guided reading should last about 15–20 minutes per group throughout the year, but independent reading should start at around 10–15 minutes per session at the beginning of the year and extend to 20–25 minutes as reading stamina increases later in the year.

Students who complete the units of study in kindergarten and first grade should have a strong foundational literacy base. They should be members of the reading and writing community ready to master the units of study introduced in second grade.

Grade 1 Writing Units

Functional Writing

Essential Skill

Students will understand that we write in different forms for different purposes.

Materials

- Samples of functional writing (invitations, recipes, menus, etc.)
- Templates for writing, such as invitations, grocery lists, thank-you cards, and event posters (see Appendix A)
- Three-column chart drawn on chart paper, with columns labeled Student, Recipient, and Purpose
- Reference chart with sample templates of functional writing
- Various types of blank paper, blank notecards, invitations, etc.
- Hanging shoe holder with compartments
- Trade books focusing on functional writing (see Suggested Texts)

Purpose

Immersion

1. In preparation for the lesson bring in various samples of functional writing, such as directions, signs and labels, recipes, menus, certificates, thank-you cards, postcards, invitations, posters that outline rules and procedures, lists, notes, notices, signs, and charts. Explain that different types of functional writing have different purposes, have different formats, and provide different information that must be included in the writing for it to be effective.

2. Have students sort the samples by type and leave the different types in labeled baskets on a table or in a learning center for examination.

3. On subsequent days read trade books that focus on functional writing (see Suggested Texts).

Collecting

4. Create templates for several types of writing, focusing especially on grocery lists, invitations, thank-you cards, and event posters (see Appendix A).

5. Model writing in these different forms and explain the importance of the structure and content of each piece of writing. Explain how the content is crucial to informing the reader.

6. Ask students to try writing different pieces using the templates.

Choosing and Developing an Idea

7. Create a three-column chart with columns labeled Student, Recipient, and Purpose (see Figure 9). List each student's name on the chart in the first column, then write the name of the person to whom they have chosen to write in the second column, and write the purpose for the correspondence in the third column. (If a student chooses to write a list, leave the second column blank.)

8. During writers' workshop, confer with students individually or in small groups (if several students are working on the same type of writing) about the information they are including in their pieces.

9. During this time the students may choose to try different forms of functional writing.

Drafting

10. Create a reference chart with sample templates for students to refer to during drafting. This may include a template for an invitation, a grocery list, or a poster advertising an upcoming event (see Appendix A).

11. Have students work on the type of writing stated next to their names on the three-column chart.

Figure 9. Functional Writing Chart

Student	Recipient	Purpose
Michael Smith	Simon Craft	Invite a friend to a party
Tara Taylor	Jenny McCabe	Thank-you card for a birthday gift

Revising

12. Discuss with students ways to make a piece more interesting in order to get a reader's attention.

13. Ask students to share their writing with a partner and decide how to make their piece more interesting by adding a picture or caption.

Editing

14. Have the students correct high-frequency words that are displayed on individual sheets or on a class chart or word wall (see Appendix B for Grade 1 High-Frequency Word List).

15. During this unit of study, help students correct as many words as possible. Explain that for a reader to get the proper information, this type of writing needs to be as correct as possible.

Follow-Up Activities

• During the year have students write invitations; create posters; or send notes home for class parties, trips, events, or celebrations.

• Create a classroom post office by labeling the compartments of a hanging shoe holder with the name of each student in the class. Students can write to one another and then place the notes, invitations, and so forth in the compartments.

• Place note paper, postcards, or invitations in all the learning centers in the room to encourage correspondence.

Assessment

Students will demonstrate an awareness of some different forms and functions writing can take.

• Throughout the year ask the students to create invitations, posters, lists, etc. Check to see if they understand what information is needed in each type of writing to make it functional for the reader.

• Interactively create posters, invitations, lists, and so forth for various events taking place during the school year. During the discussions, take note of the information students suggest so you can determine if additional lessons are required.

• Create a simple rubric with the class so students can self-evaluate their products.

Suggested Texts

Hoban, T. (1987). *I read signs.* New York: HarperCollins.

Stewart, S. (2000). *The gardener.* New York: Farrar, Straus and Giroux.

Sturges, P. (1999). *The little red hen makes a pizza.* New York: Penguin.

Williams, V.B. (1999). *Stringbean's trip to the shining sea.* New York: HarperCollins.

[handwritten note: Class Diary (Journal) another Unit? 1st of year TO Build Community]

Letter Writing

[handwritten: 2]

Essential Skill

Students will understand the purposes for writing a friendly letter.

Materials

• Samples of friendly letters donated by teacher and students

• Three-column chart drawn on chart paper, with columns labeled Student, Recipient, and Purpose

• Grade 1 High-Frequency Word List (see Appendix B)

• Trade books focusing on letter writing (see Suggested Texts)

Procedure

Immersion

1. Together with students, bring in letters from home to share with the class. Have a discussion about what makes each letter special, why you enjoyed reading it, and what information the letters contain.

2. Discuss the purposes for writing a friendly letter:

   To find out information about someone or something

   To share information about someone or something

   To share good or bad news

   To share your feelings about someone or something

   To make a request

3. With the class, compose a letter based on a class need. For example, write to the custodian requesting more paper towels in the room.

4. Follow up by reading trade books in which letter writing is key to the story line (see Suggested Texts).

Collecting

5. Ask students to create a personal list of people to whom they would like to write letters.

*[handwritten note: Class Letter * of the week]*

6. Create a template for letter writing.

7. Model how to write a letter using the template.

8. Have students write one or two letters over several days.

Choosing and Developing an Idea

9. Review the structure of a friendly letter introduced in kindergarten: date, opening, body, closing.

10. Create a three-column chart with columns labeled Student, Recipient, and Purpose. Ask students to whom they would like to write and why. Write this information next to each name (see Figure 10). Consider suggesting some fanciful recipients, too, such as the tooth fairy, Santa Claus, or a favorite book character.

Drafting

11. Write another class letter with students for a different purpose than the first shared writing.

12. Display the class letters for student reference.

13. Ask the students to write letters to the recipients listed next to their names on the three-column chart.

Revising

14. Share a prewritten letter in which the information contained in the body of the letter is randomly placed, causing the letter to be difficult to understand. Reread the letter numbering the parts in the order they should occur if the letter is to make sense. Rearrange the letter accordingly and reread it checking for clarity (see Figure 11).

15. Students will reread their letters and rearrange the information if necessary to make sure their letters make sense.

Editing

16. Have students check spelling of high-frequency words (see Appendix B for Grade 1 High-Frequency Word List).

17. Help with basic editing, explaining that this type of public writing should be as correct as possible.

Figure 10. Letter Writing Chart

Student	Recipient	Purpose
Jose Fernandez	Grandma	Ask her to visit at Christmas
Susan Olsen	Big Sister	Tell her I won the spelling contest

Figure 11. Scrambled Letter

Dear Aunt Sylvia,

Write to me soon.
We went home and ate cake.
We saw monkeys. I had a good birthday.
Mom and Dad took me. We went to the zoo.

Love,
Robert

Follow-Up Activities

- Continue to write letters, interactively or as a shared class experience. These letters can be to favorite authors or school personnel.
- Suggest to parents that they become pen pals with their children in order to facilitate ongoing written communication.

Assessment

Students will be able to recognize and write a friendly letter containing information relevant to the intent of the correspondence.

- After drafts are revised and edited, confer with students individually. Ask about the intended recipient and the reason for writing the letter. Based on the conference, check the written piece to assess if the contents match the student's intent.

Suggested Texts

Ada, A.F. (1997). *Dear Peter Rabbit.* New York: Simon & Schuster.
Ada, A.F. (2005). *Yours truly, Goldilocks.* New York: Simon & Schuster.
Harrison, J. (1995). *Dear bear.* Minneapolis, MN: Carolrhoda Books.
Lobel, A. (1979). *Frog and Toad together.* New York: HarperCollins.

Writing Personal Narrative 3

Essential Skill

Students will understand that a personal narrative has a structure and this structure helps the reader to make sense of the story.

Materials

- Several familiar texts, some with a clear story structure and at least one list book (see Suggested Texts)

- Three-column chart drawn on chart paper, with columns labeled Beginning, Middle, and End
- Sheet of paper folded in three sections labeled Beginning, Middle, and End—one for each student
- Two-column chart drawn on chart paper, with columns labeled Name and My Story Idea
- Grade 1 High-Frequency Word List (see Appendix B)
- Grade 1 Editing Checklist (see Appendix B)

Procedure

Immersion

1. On the first day, read a simple list book from beginning to end. Then reread the list book starting from different points in the book. Explain that a list book can be read in any order and it will still make sense because it is not a story and therefore does not need to have a beginning, middle, or end.

2. Choose a text (preferably a familiar one) that has a clear story structure (beginning, middle, and end). Say, "Today we are going to learn about the structure of a story, or how the author decides to put the story together so it makes sense to the reader." Explain again that a list book can be read in any order, but if a writer is telling a story it needs to have a beginning, a middle, and an end to make sense.

3. Read the complete story. Then reread the story, pointing out the beginning, the middle, and the end of the story. After finishing the story, ask the class what would happen if you read the story starting in the middle or starting at the end. Make sure students understand that a story written within a narrative structure must start at the beginning and continue in sequential order, otherwise the story won't make sense.

4. Repeat the lesson using different stories, continuing to read and point out the beginning, the middle point, and the end of the story.

5. Read a story, such as *Babushka's Doll* (Polacco, 1995). Then create a chart containing three sections labeled Beginning, Middle, and End. Brainstorm with the students and then write a few sentences in each section, summarizing the major parts of the story (see Figure 12). The writing can be done interactively or solely by you. The interactive experience is a whole-group shared writing experience generally done on chart paper. The students help to compose the text, and then volunteers take turns with the teacher writing the

Figure 12. Beginning, Middle, and End Chart for Narrative Writing

Beginning	Middle	End
Natasha was at her grandmother's farm. She was not being nice to her grandmother. She kept ordering her grandmother to do things.	Natasha's grandmother gave her a doll to play with and then left to go to town. The doll came to life and started ordering Natasha around. Natasha didn't like being treated so mean.	When her grandmother came back, Natasha gave her back the doll and started acting nicely toward her grandmother. Her grandmother asked if she wanted to play with the doll again, and Natasha said, "No, once is enough!"

text or "sharing the pen." The goal is to practice using sound–symbol correspondence when writing words, reinforce knowledge of high-frequency words, and increase competency in the use of punctuation and capitalization. Continue to stress the idea that the structure allows the story to make sense.

6. Choose several touchstone texts that are strong examples of everyday events that occur in peoples' lives (see Suggested Texts). During read-aloud time or shared reading time, discuss with students how authors get ideas for the books they write. Then explain that authors think about details to add to make a book more interesting. Finally explain that authors organize these ideas and details by deciding what should go in the beginning, the middle, or the end of the book. The organization is what helps the book to make sense.

7. Model telling a story from your own life, stressing the beginning, middle, and end as you tell the story. Explain that authors get many ideas from the things that happen to them in their own lives. Ask students to share personal stories, stressing that they should remember to tell the story by organizing the events in the story by what happens in the beginning, the middle, and the end.

8. Create a form divided into three sections labeled Beginning, Middle, and End. Have students write life stories by filling in each section with a sketch.

9. Have students use the sketch to tell their stories.

Collecting

10. Have students start a list of possible "life story" topics.

11. Ask students to talk with family members about events that might make good stories to write about.

12. Ask students to bring in photos or artifacts that can help them get ideas for stories to add to their lists.

13. Hand out sheets of paper folded in thirds, with each section labeled Beginning, Middle, and End. Have the students choose one story and then sketch the beginning, middle, and end in the appropriate section of the paper. During whole-class share time, ask a few students to talk about their stories using their sketch as a guide. Repeat several times over the next few days.

14. In a small group or in partners, have students take turns telling stories from their sketches. Have the other students ask questions and make suggestions about possible details to add to the story. Also, after each story is told, have the storyteller ask if the story had a beginning, a middle, and an end and if the story made sense. While the stories are being told, circulate around the room checking on the groups or partnerships and joining in on the questioning.

Choosing and Developing an Idea

15. Have students choose one or more of the stories from their sketches to write about. Instruct them to structure the story around a beginning, a middle, and end as they did in their sketches. Encourage them to add at least one interesting detail in each section.

Drafting

16. Create a two-column chart, labeling the left column Name and the right column My Story Idea. Ask students to look over their collection of stories and choose a "life story" to draft. Write the story ideas next to each name on the chart (see Figure 13). At this time introduce the term *personal narrative*. Explain that a personal narrative is a story from your life that has a narrative structure, which means it has a beginning, a middle, and an end; this structure holds the story together and helps it to make sense.

17. Instruct students to write their personal narratives initially focusing on structuring the piece with a beginning, a middle, and an end.

Revising

18. Have students reread their drafts to make sure their pieces have a beginning, a middle, and an end. Ask them to reread the piece to a partner to make sure it makes sense.

Figure 13. Personal Narrative Story Idea Chart

Name	My Story Idea
Louis	Getting a new puppy
Aaliyah	My baby sister

19. Ask students to reread their draft a second time, making one small move to improve the piece, such as changing the word *said* to the word *shouted*.

Editing

20. Place a Grade 1 High-Frequency Word List (see Appendix B) in students' writing folders or notebooks. Ask students to edit their writing by checking that high-frequency words are spelled correctly.

21. Emphasize punctuation by asking students to check for periods in their pieces.

22. Together with students, create a short editing checklist (see Appendix B for Grade 1 Editing Checklist) to keep in their folders or notebooks.

Follow-Up Activities

• Continue to write personal narratives focusing on the importance of writing within a narrative structure.

• Discuss and model how to write a story around one important moment occurring within a bigger event. For example, the big event is going to an amusement park, but the narrative is about going on the roller coaster.

• Focus the writing lesson on improving word choice. For example, create a chart and list all the other words we can use in place of *said* (*replied*, *grumbled*, and *yelled*).

• Introduce the use of quotation marks in the narrative to get students familiar with the concept of dialogue.

• Later in the year, look to improve the quality of the different sections in a narrative. For example just work on creating a "Bright Beginning," a "Meaty Middle," or an "Exciting End."

Assessment

Students will demonstrate the ability to write a simple personal narrative containing a beginning, a middle, and an end with some details.

• Together with students, review a simple rubric to decide if a piece is satisfactory or if it needs more revision and editing. The rubric should reflect the purpose of the study. For example, the first rubric should evaluate the structure of a piece (see Figure 14).

• During conferences use the rubric to decide if the piece is ready to publish or if it needs to be revised.

Figure 14. Personal Narrative Writing Rubric

Great	OK	Needs More Work

The story has a beginning, a middle, and an end.	The story needs more work in the beginning, the middle, or the end.	The story needs a beginning, a middle, or an end.
The story has interesting details in each section.	The story has some details but would be better with more details.	The story needs details.
The story makes sense.	The story makes some sense.	The story doesn't make sense.

- Keep all of the drafting attempts for several pieces in order to assess growth throughout the year.

Suggested Texts

Barbour, K. (1990). *Little Nino's pizzeria.* San Diego, CA: Harcourt.

Fleming, D. (2000). *The everything book.* New York: Henry Holt.

Jonas, A. (1987). *Reflections.* New York: HarperCollins.

Polacco, P. (1995). *Babushka's doll.* New York: Simon & Schuster.

Rockwell, A. (2000). *Ferryboat ride!* New York: Random House.

Tarpley, N.A. (2001). *I love my hair!* Boston: Little, Brown.

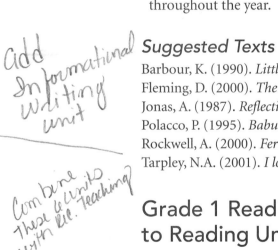

Grade 1 Reading and Response to Reading Units

Story Structure

Essential Skill

Students will understand that a story has a beginning, a middle, and an end and will be able to demonstrate this knowledge by retelling a story in sequence.

Materials

- Several three-column charts drawn on chart paper, with columns labeled Beginning, Middle, and End

• Several trade books with a clear structure (see Suggested Texts)

Procedure

Modeling

1. Begin the lesson by reviewing that a story has a structure (a beginning, a middle, and an end) and this structure allows the story to make sense. Read a story with a strong structure (see Suggested Texts) and then divide chart paper into three sections labeled Beginning, Middle, and End. Identify each section of the story and explain that if you had to write down or retell this story to someone who didn't know it, you would have to pick out the most important ideas in each section in order for the story to make sense. Proceed to summarize one section of the story at a time and write the summary in the appropriate box on the chart. Then retell the story using the chart as a guide (see Figure 15).

2. On subsequent days, retell different stories without using the chart but continue to identify each section of the story as it is being told. Say, "In the beginning of the story..., then in the middle of the story..., and finally at the end of the story...." Do not request student input at this time.

Guided Reading

3. After the initial lesson read several more stories during shared reading or read-aloud time, asking for student assistance to summarize the story and fill in the sections of the chart. (This can also be done interactively, with students taking turns "sharing the pen.")

Figure 15. Retelling Chart

Title: *The Carrot Seed* by Ruth Krauss (1945)

Beginning

A little boy planted a carrot seed.

Middle

His family told him it wouldn't come up.

End

The carrot seed did come up and grew into an enormous carrot.

4. On subsequent days, in small groups or with partners have students retell either classroom read-aloud stories or independently read stories to each other. Reinforce the idea that stories must be told starting at the beginning and progressing to the end in order for the stories to make sense.

Independent Reading

5. During independent reading time, when you are conferring with students, ask them to retell the stories they have read independently.

6. Pair up students after independent reading sessions and have them retell to each other the stories they have read.

Follow-Up Activities

• During readers' workshop, model how to retell a read-aloud story pointing out the beginning, the middle, and the end of the story. Emphasize how you chose the points to include in the retelling. Demonstrate how to select major points of interest and eliminate minor points. Have students retell other read-aloud stories, pointing out the beginning, the middle, and the end of each story.

• During writers' workshop, have students write their own story using Story Structure Boxes (see Appendix A).

• On sentence strips, write sentences from a story read during guided reading. Using a pocket chart or flannel board, have students put the story in correct order by placing the strips in rows labeled Beginning, Middle, and End.

• Assign small groups of students one section of a familiar story to illustrate and then summarize in one or two sentences. Have the groups join together and retell the story in the correct sequence.

Assessment

Students will demonstrate their knowledge of story structure by sequentially retelling a story, centering on the most important ideas in the beginning, the middle, and the end of the story.

• Select several different read-aloud stories that demonstrate a strong story structure. Each day after a whole-class read-aloud session, have individual students retell the story. The story can be told to the whole group or to you during a conference.

• Students who do not demonstrate mastery should be grouped together and continue practicing retelling stories during guided reading sessions or independent conferences.

Suggested Texts

Baylor, B. (1985). *Everybody needs a rock*. New York: Simon & Schuster.

Johnson, A. (2000). *Down the winding road*. New York: Dorling Kindersley.

Krauss, R. (1945). *The carrot seed*. New York: HarperCollins.

Pilkey, D. (1999). *The paperboy*. Danbury, CT: Orchard Books.

Rylant, C. (2000). *In November*. San Diego, CA: Harcourt.

Story Elements 2

Essential Skill

Students will be able to verbally define a story's elements and explain how these elements help the story to make sense.

Materials

- Familiar trade book (see Suggested Texts)
- Three-column chart drawn on chart paper, with columns labeled Characters, Setting, and Events
- Story Elements Chart (see Appendix A)

Procedure

Modeling

1. Reread a familiar story, then say, "When we think about a story after we read it and before we write about or retell it, we first have to think about its structure. We think about what happened at the beginning, the middle, and the end of the story. We know that if we tell the story out of order it won't make sense. Today, I'm going to read *The Gingerbread Boy*. After I read I'm going to think about some other important things that help me to understand the story better." Read the whole story aloud and then say, "I think knowing the characters helps me to understand the story better."

2. Introduce the three-column chart and in the first column write the heading Characters and list the characters underneath. Next say, "I think knowing where the story takes place helps me to understand the story better. *The Gingerbread Boy* takes place on a farm. This is called the setting." Write the heading Setting on the chart and list the setting (list all of the major settings if the setting shifts in a story, but for the initial readings choose stories in which the setting is constant). Finally say, "Several things happen in this story.

First, the gingerbread boy jumps out of the oven and runs away, then everyone chases him, and finally he gets tricked and eaten by a fox. These things are called the events, and the events help me to understand the story better." Write the heading Events on the chart and then number and list the events from the story in the order that they happened. Explain that the details you've written on the chart are called story elements and that these elements help us to understand a story better (see Figure 16).

3. Repeat this lesson on subsequent days using several new stories. Include some of the other story element terms, such as *plot*, *problem*, and *solution*. Define and explain each element as it is introduced and add these as new columns on the chart.

Guided Reading

4. After read-aloud time or shared reading, draw a simple Story Elements Chart (see Appendix A) on chart paper and with input from the students list the story elements.

Independent Reading

5. During independent reading, ask students to list the story elements on sticky notes in the book they are reading and then share their notes with the class. Each element should be done separately for the first few weeks. For example, list only the characters on sticky notes the first week, then the next week list only the settings, and then finally list the events.

6. When students are proficient at identifying the elements, the Story Elements Chart can be used during independent reading time as an independent activity to follow up the reading of a "just-right" book.

Figure 16. Story Elements Chart

Characters	Setting	Events
The old man	Farm	The old man and the old woman bake a gingerbread boy.
The old woman		
The gingerbread boy		The gingerbread boy jumps out of the oven and runs away.
Cow		
Horse		All of the people and animals chase him.
Pig		
Fox		The fox tricks and eats him.

Figure 17. Story Elements Sort

Title: *The Little Red Hen*
Words/Phrases: *chicks, cat, farm, goat, mill, grind flour, bake bread, do it herself*

Characters	Settings	Problems	Solution
chicks	farm	grind flour	do it herself
cat	mill	bake bread	
goat			

Follow-Up Activities

• After hearing or reading several different stories, students can choose a character they like, dislike, or connect with. In oral or written form they can explain their reasons for choosing this character.

• After reading two stories during read-aloud time, use a Venn diagram or Y-chart (see Appendix A) to compare and contrast the characters, settings, or events between two books. Discuss the conclusions that can be drawn from the stories, focusing on the similarities between the two stories. For example, ask, "What conclusions can we draw about the characters in *The Three Billy Goats Gruff* and *The Three Little Pigs*?"

• Do a Story Elements Sort by writing on index cards certain relevant words and phrases from a story that you'll read aloud. Create a chart with columns labeled Characters, Settings, Problems, and Solution and, before reading, have students place the cards into appropriate columns (see Figure 17). Read the story aloud, then check to see if the elements were placed in the correct columns. This activity can be done with the whole class using a pocket chart and then individually using a worksheet.

Assessment

Students will demonstrate the ability to identify the elements of a story and orally retell the story using the elements to help the story make sense.

• Each day, choose a different story to read during read-aloud time. Students will listen to the stories as a group and chart the characters, setting, and events. During independent reading, confer with the students and ask them to retell the story using the elements as a guide.

Suggested Texts

Crews, D. (1996). *Shortcut*. New York: HarperCollins.
Galdone, P. (1981). *The three billy goats Gruff*. Boston: Houghton Mifflin.

Galdone, P. (1983). *The gingerbread boy.* Boston: Houghton Mifflin.

Williams, V.B. (1991). *Cherries and cherry pits.* New York: HarperCollins.

Change Over Time

Essential Skill

Students will be able to recognize the events that cause a change in character.

Materials

- Several trade books that demonstrate a character or object changing over time (see Suggested Texts)
- Timelines drawn on chart paper labeled Beginning and End, with space for at least three events in the middle

Procedure

Modeling

1. Read aloud a story that clearly demonstrates an object or character changing over time, such as *The Little House* (Burton, 1978). After reading the entire story discuss the characteristics of a character or object (such as "house" in this example) at the beginning and then again at the end of the story. Draw a simple timeline on the board and fill in the characteristics and precipitous events on the timeline that contribute to the change (see Figure 18). Wrap up by saying, "I realize now that when I read a story certain events that take place will cause the characters to change, and I have to pay attention to the events that might be causing the change."

2. Repeat this lesson using different stories, but at this point do not solicit input from the students.

Guided Reading

3. Using a new text, model the lesson once again, but this time elicit the necessary information from the students to fill in the timeline. Repeat two or three times with other new texts and timelines.

Independent Reading

4. During independent reading conferences, ask students to explain what a character is like at the beginning of a book. Ask if the character is changing as the story continues and, once the student has completed the book, ask how the character was at the end of the story. Also ask students to explain what caused the changes.

Figure 18. Story Timeline

Beginning—Little house happy in the country but curious about the city

Event 1—Roads and houses built around her; not sure if she liked it

Event 2—Skyscrapers, trains, and subways built next to and under her; sad and lonely

Event 3—Great granddaughter of original owner bought house and moved her to country again

End—Little house happy again; no longer curious about the city

Follow-Up Activities

• Repeat this lesson using stories that demonstrate changes across different story elements. For example, discuss change over time in a story in which the setting changes.

• Repeat this lesson using a story that demonstrates the story line changing from the beginning to the end. For example, the book *The Secret Shortcut* (Teague, 1999) begins like realistic fiction and changes to fantasy because of certain events that take place. Continue to emphasize the causative factors for change during discussion around the story.

• During writers' workshop, ask students to experiment with character change in their story drafts.

Assessment

Students will be able to recognize that change has occurred either to a character or to a story, and they will be able to point to some of the reasons for the change.

• In preparation for this assessment create a simple timeline. Read a story to the class. Ask students to write or draw how the character was at the beginning of the story and at the end of the story, as well as two or three events that might have caused the character change. A good text for this assessment is *Babushka's Doll* (Polacco, 1995).

Suggested Texts

Aliki. (1987). *The two of them.* New York: HarperCollins.

Burton, V.L. (1978). *The little house.* Boston: Houghton Mifflin.

Duvoisin, R. (2000). *Petunia.* New York: Knopf.

Henkes, K. (1998). *Jessica.* New York: HarperCollins.

Polacco, P. (1995). *Babushka's doll.* New York: Simon & Schuster.

Teague, M. (1999). *The secret shortcut.* New York: Scholastic

Voirst, J. (1987). *Alexander and the terrible, horrible, no good, very bad day.* New York: Simon & Schuster.

Characteristics of Genre

Essential Skill

Students will understand that within a given genre there are different categories of the same type of text; for instance, fictitious text can be folk tale or mystery.

Materials

- Several trade books from different genres and a variety of books from within a genre (see Suggested Texts)
- Two-column chart drawn on chart paper, with columns labeled Genre: Fiction and Characteristics
- Three-column chart drawn on chart paper, with columns labeled Genre: Fiction, Type of Fiction, and Characteristics

Procedure

Modeling

1. Create a chart with columns labeled Genre: Fiction and Characteristics. Together with students, read several different fiction books and write the titles under the fiction heading. Then write the general characteristics under the heading Characteristics (see Figure 19).

2. Select a few familiar fiction books that fall into categories such as mystery, folk tale, and plays. Read a portion of one type of text, then hold up another different type of text and say, "I know both of these books are fiction because they fit the characteristics we talked about and put on the chart. However, these books are not the same type of book, and even though they fit the main characteristics of the genre they have some of their own characteristics, too. Each genre can have different types of stories in it." On the three-column chart, under the Genre: Fiction column, write the title of the book; then write the type of fiction in the middle column and list some characteristics in the right column (see Figure 20).

Figure 19. Characteristics of Genre Chart

Genre: Fiction	Characteristics
Title: *The Magic Fish* (Littledale, 1989)	1. The story is made up.
Title: *The Carrot Seed* (Krauss, 1945)	2. Sometimes animals or objects talk.
Title: *Chicka Chicka Boom Boom* (Martin & Archambault, 1992)	3. Silly things can happen.
Title: *Brown Bear, Brown Bear, What Do You See?* (Martin & Carle, 1992)	

Figure 20. Categories of Fiction Chart

Genre: Fiction	Type of Fiction	Characteristics
Title: *Anansi and the Moss-Covered Rock* (Kimmel, 1990)	Folk tale	Has talking animals in the story Usually explains an event or phenomenon happening in an unusual way
Title: *25 Just-Right Plays for Emergent Readers* (Pugliano-Martin, 1999)	Play	Usually has different characters Has characters with parts
Title: *High-Rise Private Eyes #1* (Rylant, 2002)	Mystery	Has an important event occur Has characters who figure out how it happens

Guided Reading

3. Continue to read from different categories of fiction. With student participation, identify the type of fiction of each text and list some characteristics that the text exhibits that prompted its placement in that category. Emphasize that several different types of stories are contained within a genre and discuss the characteristics that set apart each category within fiction. (For instance, within fiction, there are fairy tales, realistic fiction, and mysteries.)

Independent Reading

4. Set up genre baskets labeled with the name of the genre but containing texts from the different categories that were introduced during Modeling. For several days ask students to read within the specific genres. Duplicate the Categories of Genre chart onto individual sheets and have the students fill in the correct information. (Note: If students have difficulty listing the characteristics, they can copy them from the large class chart. Identifying the category is what is important here.)

Follow-Up Activities

- Demonstrate sorting books in genre baskets into separate baskets based on category. (For example, sort a fiction basket into mysteries, plays, and so forth.) In small groups have students sort and label genre baskets into separate baskets based on categories to place in the classroom library. Throughout the year, read-aloud and shared reading titles should be added to the baskets.

- Repeat sorting categories into separate baskets, paying attention to the types of books that fall within a genre; create a fantasy basket, a folk tale basket, etc.

- Create a Grade 1 Reading Log (see Appendix B) and ask students to list the genre and category of the books they read.

- Create a recommendation board, listing books by genre and category. Have students write a recommendation about a book they have read during independent reading time and place the summary under the title on the board.

- During writers' workshop, have students rewrite a draft in a different genre. For example, rewrite a simple narrative story into a poem.

Assessment

Students will demonstrate knowledge of the different categories of text that exist within a genre by classifying different types of text by their characteristics.

- Ask the children about genre during independent reading conferences. Question what genre and specifically what category of text within a genre they are currently reading and what genres they have read in the past. Ask students what characteristics in the text helped them to identify the genre and category.

Suggested Texts

Drama

Pugliano-Martin, C. (1999). *25 just-right plays for emergent readers*. New York: Scholastic.

Fairy Tale

Littledale, F. (1989). *The magic fish*. New York: Scholastic.

Marshall, J. (1993). *Red Riding Hood*. New York: Penguin.

Fiction

Krauss, R. (1945). *The carrot seed*. New York: HarperCollins.

Martin, B., Jr, & Archambault, J. (1992). *Chicka chicka boom boom*. New York: Simon & Schuster.

Martin, B., Jr, & Carle, E. (1992). *Brown bear, brown bear, what do you see?* New York: Holt, Rinehart and Winston.

Rylant, C. (2002). *High-rise private eyes series #1.* New York: HarperCollins.

Folk Tale

Kimmel, E. (1990). *Anansi and the moss-covered rock.* New York: Holiday House.

Newton-John, O. (1999). *A pig tale.* London: Aladdin.

Poetry

Graham, J.B. (2003). *Flicker flash.* Boston: Houghton Mifflin.

Realistic Fiction

Havill, J. (1989). *Jamaica tag-along.* Boston: Houghton Mifflin.

Compare/Contrast/Conclude 5

Essential Skill

Students will understand that opinions are formed and supported by the similarities that exist between texts.

Materials

- Two familiar texts with strong similarities among characters, plot, or main idea (see Suggested Texts)
- T-chart drawn on chart paper

Procedure

Modeling

1. In preparation for this lesson choose two texts with strong similarities (for example, *Cinderella* and *Sleeping Beauty*) among the characters, plot, or main idea. Read one text and review how to retell a story focusing on the major points in the beginning, the middle, and the end. On the following day read the second text, again focusing on the major points in the beginning, the middle, and the end of the story. Then say, "I noticed in both stories the main characters were treated poorly. The authors of both books didn't tell us in words that the characters were treated poorly, but I can tell by some of the things that happened in the story that they wanted us to know this. I am going to show you how I can write down the evidence to prove my thinking about the characters in both books." Draw a T-chart on chart paper and model how to go through the book to fill in the T-chart with text evidence to support your thinking (see Figure 21).

Figure 21. Compare/Contrast T-Chart

Cinderella and Sleeping Beauty were treated poorly.	
Story 1 (Cinderella)	Story 2 (Sleeping Beauty)
Cinderella had a lot of chores to do.	Sleeping Beauty had to hide in the woods.
The stepsisters were mean to Cinderella and didn't let her go to the ball.	Sleeping Beauty couldn't be with her family.
Cinderella didn't have nice clothes.	An evil curse was put on Sleeping Beauty so she couldn't wake up.

2. Repeat this lesson several times, pointing out the similarities between two texts; however, each time focus on a different story element (for example, compare similar settings).

Guided Reading

3. Use the same text as in the first lesson, but this time formulate another opinion. Say, "I noticed in these books that the characters liked to help others." Form small groups and ask the students to see if they can find evidence to support this opinion. The groups can meet, decide on the evidence in both texts, and orally present their evidence. After the groups have presented, chart the evidence by deciding on the most important or the most common evidence found across groups.

4. Repeat this activity several times throughout the year.

Independent Reading

5. Ask partners or small groups of students to independently read several texts that have a common theme. After reading the texts have the partners or groups meet to decide on a common opinion about the texts. Then have them find evidence in the text they read to support this opinion. Have the partners or groups share with the whole class.

Follow-Up Activities

• Later in the year repeat using a T-chart after reading nonfiction text. Introduce two texts on the same topic, such as insects. Pose a question for inquiry, such as "Are insects helpful or harmful in a garden?" Write the question at the top of the T-chart and ask students to recall relevant information to substantiate each opinion. Write their responses on the chart.

• Select a folk tale or fairy tale and a nonfiction text written about the same type of creature, such as a spider. Use a T-chart to record evidence from both texts to answer the question "Are spiders smart and tricky creatures?"

Assessment

Students will demonstrate an understanding that multiple texts in different genres can contain evidence or information to form or support an idea.

• Pose a simple question to the class, such as "Do animals in folk tales usually do smart or not-so-smart things?" Read several folk tales containing animals. During small-group guided reading or individual conference time, ask the students what they think, and ask them to recall places in the text to back up their opinions. Take note if they are able to select evidence to support their opinions.

Suggested Texts

Blair, E. (2004). *Sleeping beauty*. Minnetonka, MN: Capstone.

Cowley, J. (2006). *Red-eyed tree frog*. New York: Scholastic.

Johnson, A. (2000). *Down the winding road*. New York: Dorling Kindersley.

Lionni, L. (1973). *Swimmy*. New York: Knopf.

Marshall, J. (2001). *Cinderella*. New York: Penguin.

Pfeffer, W. (1994). *From tadpole to frog*. New York: HarperCollins.

Rylant, C. (1993). *The relatives came*. New York: Simon & Schuster.

Recognizing the Main Idea

Essential Skill

Students will understand that a story has a main idea and a supporting structure (details) that connects to the main idea

Materials

• Several familiar fiction texts (see Suggested Texts)
• Story Web (see Appendix A) drawn on chart paper

Procedure

Modeling

1. Begin this lesson by telling students that many times when we like a story or book, we enjoy talking about the book or recommending the book to someone else. Then tell them you are going to model how to tell a story to someone who doesn't know the story or book you are recommending. Say, "The first thing we have to think about when we are talking about a book is the main idea, or what the story is mostly about. Next, we need to think about what happens in the beginning, the middle, and the end of the story. We need

to pay attention to the main things that happen in each part and some details that make what happens in each part either more clear or more interesting." Read a new story aloud, completely and without stopping for discussion. Once completed, discuss your thoughts about the main idea. Then point out key events in the beginning, middle, and end of the story that support your opinion of the main idea. Wrap up by saying, "All the things or the details that happened in each part of the story helped me to figure out what the main idea was."

2. On the following day, using the same story, draw a story web on the board and say, "Yesterday I retold the story to you, but today I decided to use a story web to help us write down the main idea and the details connected to the main idea." Write Main Idea in the large center cell of the web, then briefly write what the story was mostly about in that cell. Then label the three connecting cells Beginning, Middle, and End and summarize in those cells the main events from the beginning, middle, and end of the story. Finally, under each of the three cells draw connecting cells and include a few details that clarify or support each event (see Figure 22 and Appendix A).

Guided Reading

3. Repeat creating a story web several times, reading a new story each time. In each successive lesson, elicit from the students the main idea; the main points in the beginning, the middle, and the end of the story; and some supporting details. Also have students retell the story using the story web as a guide.

Independent Reading

4. Select students to retell their independent reading books to the whole class or to their partners during shared reading time. When the students retell, stress that they should be stating the main idea and supplying details to back up the main idea.

Follow-Up Activities

• After students listen to a book, share a book during guided reading, or independently read a book, have them complete a Main Idea Summary Sheet stating what the book was mostly about and including several details that back up the main idea (see Appendix A).

• Coach students to do a book talk using the Main Idea Summary sheet. This can be from an independent reading book, guided reading book, or read-aloud book.

Figure 22. Story Web Showing Main Idea

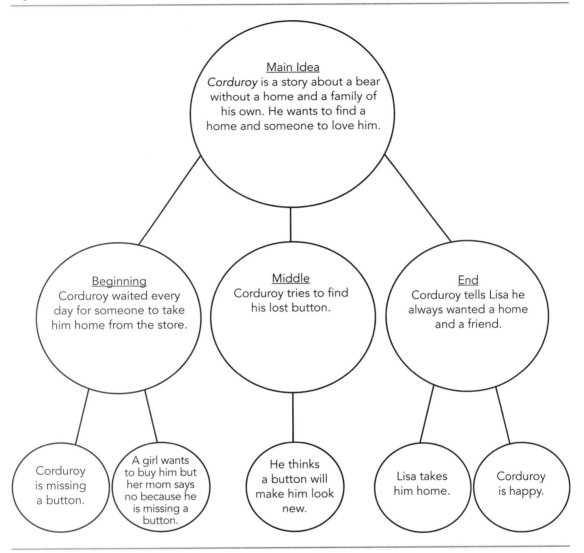

• Create a blank story web and ask students to complete it for homework using an independent reading book or a story that was read to them at home.

Assessment

Students will demonstrate the ability to retell a story around the main idea and be able to support the idea with relevant details.

• After a read-aloud, guided reading, or independent reading session, ask individual students to retell the story they just experienced. First ask, "What was the main idea of the story?" and then ask, "What were the most important things that happened in the beginning, the middle, and the end of the story?"

Suggested Texts

Carle, E. (1996). *The grouchy ladybug.* New York: HarperCollins.

Fox, M. (1997). *Sophie.* San Diego, CA: Harcourt.

Freeman, D. (1968). *Corduroy.* New York: Viking Press.

Kraus, R. (1994). *Leo the late bloomer.* New York: HarperCollins.

Zolotow, C. (1968). *My friend John.* New York: HarperCollins.

CHAPTER 4

Grade 2: Moving Right Along

Students and teachers in grade 2 should be ready to begin mastery instruction very early in the school year because students are entering grade 2 with prior knowledge and experience with a balanced literacy framework. They also are familiar with the terminology, structures, and expectations that are part of the units of study provided in the mastery lessons.

The major goals for grade 2 students are to move toward greater independence using the reading and writing strategies that have been taught in previous grades and to take more responsibility for their learning. They will be making more choices in the types of writing they do and the types of books they read. The units of study provided in this chapter will help move students toward these goals.

Students will practice writing postcards and friendly letters. They will also take more responsibility for editing their work using a high-frequency word wall or word chart and an editing checklist as a guide. They will continue to share stories from their lives by writing personal narratives, but beyond their previous experiences with focus and structure they will learn how to add relevant details to inform and entertain the reader. While in kindergarten and grade 1, students were expected to understand the form and function of these types of writings. In grade 2, students will be asked to independently write an invitation, a friendly letter, and a personal narrative.

The suggested minilessons that are part of the grade 2 writing units should take approximately 15 minutes. Sessions when students choose, develop, and draft their ideas should start at about 15 minutes but then extend to around 25–30 minutes later in the year, and this should be the case with revising and editing as well.

During reading and response to reading units, grade 2 students will use their background knowledge of story structure and story elements to deepen their reading comprehension. They will retell stories using a graphic organizer to help them focus on the main idea and supporting details. They will learn to use their knowledge of story to give an accurate retelling of a text and to use a timeline to chart the events that mark a character's change over time. They will read more extensively in different genres and record the characteristics that help them recognize these genres. They will also learn how to compare, contrast, and draw conclusions about various genres using a graphic organizer to record their thinking.

The whole-class minilessons that are part of the reading units should take approximately 20 minutes. Guided reading should last about 15–20 minutes per group throughout the year, but independent reading should start with 15-minute sessions and extend to 20–25 minute sessions as students' reading stamina increases throughout the year.

At the completion of grade 2, students should have the background knowledge and support skills necessary to meet the demands of a grade 3 curriculum. During grade 2, you will need to spend more time assessing your students, paying close attention to the levels of mastery they are achieving, because it may be necessary to review skills taught in this and at earlier grade levels to ensure that students will be able to meet the demands placed on them at higher grade levels.

Grade 2 Writing Units

Functional Writing

Essential Skill

Students will understand that different types of functional writing have different structures.

Materials

• Samples of functional writing, such as signs, advertisements, posters, postcards, etc.

• Postcard template (see Appendix A)

• Thank-you card sample (see Appendix A)

• Trade books focusing on postcard and note writing (see Suggested Texts)

Procedure

Immersion

1. Discuss with students that functional writing is writing that you get information from. It doesn't usually have a lot of details, but the details contained are crucial to the message. Functional writing is written for a specific audience, and the author generally is not known. Functional writing can be written in different ways on different types of paper. Discuss examples of

functional writing, such a signs, labels, posters, notes, invitations, advertisements, lists, certificates, directions, menus, schedules, and postcards.

2. Ask students to bring in samples of functional writing from home. Also provide samples yourself.

3. Discuss the different structures and formats functional writing takes and how these structures and formats help a writer to deliver the proper information to the reader.

4. Have students sort the available samples by format (for example, all invitations will be placed together, all menus will be placed together, etc.).

Collecting

5. Focus on postcards and notes for model lessons.

6. Create a simple two-column chart listing the characteristics of a postcard on one side and the characteristics of a note on the other. For instance, a postcard contains a quick message with few details. It is not private because the message is next to the address and available for everyone to read. A postcard usually has a photograph or drawing on the front. On the other hand, a note is written for a specific audience and the message is usually private. The writing is not conversational, however, but it is direct and to the point. Notes contain specific information.

7. Create a template for a postcard (see Appendix A) and explain where the greeting, body, closing, and address should appear.

8. Create a sample note and explain where the greeting, body, and closing appear (see Figure 23).

9. Have students try writing postcards or notes during writers' workshop or in learning centers during center time.

10. Read trade books in which functional writing, specifically postcards and notes, are central to the theme (see Suggested Texts).

Figure 23. Sample Note

Dear Mrs. Russell,

Tom was absent on May 2 because he had a cold.

Sincerely,
Mrs. Collins

Choosing and Developing an Idea

11. Students must understand that audience and purpose determine the structure or format of the writing. Ask students to choose a person with whom they would like to communicate. Then have students decide on the information they would like to share. Finally, have them choose whether a postcard or note structure would be the best way to convey the information they want to share. Emphasize that before writers begin to write they must think about the audience they are writing for and the reasons for writing.

Drafting

12. Have students write a postcard or note to a specific audience for a specific purpose.

Revising

13. Model how to focus one's writing and how to keep the writing brief and to the point.

14. Have students reread and eliminate extra or unnecessary information.

Editing

15. Explain that writing that communicates information must be as correct as possible in order for the reader to receive the proper information. Create a Grade 2 Editing Checklist (see Appendix B) to keep in students' notebooks or folders.

16. Place a copy of the Grade 2 High-Frequency Word List (see Appendix B) in student notebooks or folders, or post them on a chart or word wall for reference. Ask students to check their writing against the grade 2 high-frequency words for correct spelling.

Follow-Up Activities

- Introduce different types of notes that require specific types of information. For example, discuss the information that would be included in a note to the lunchroom staff requesting pizza for lunch on Fridays. Create templates for these types of notes and encourage students to write them.

- Place a box on your desk with blank index cards and encourage students to write postcards to different people in the school.

- Encourage student input when drafting notes to parents about class trips, requests for donations for bake sales, and so forth.

- Read school notes that are being sent home to parents. Have students assess the contents for clarity and information.

Assessment

Students will demonstrate the ability to write a simple note or postcard containing concise and accurate information.

• After students draft notes or postcards during writers' workshop, collect and assess the finished products for structure and content. Continue to collect samples throughout the year in order to assess each student's ability to write accurate notes and postcards.

Suggested Texts

Ahlberg, J., & Ahlberg, A. (2001). *The jolly postman or other people's letters*. Boston: Little, Brown.

Arnold, H. (1996). *Postcards from Mexico*. Austin, TX: Raintree.

Dawson, Z. (1995). *Postcards from China*. Austin, TX: Raintree.

Leedy, L. (1996). *Postcards from Pluto: A tour of the solar system*. New York: Holiday House.

Orloff, K.K. (2004). *I wanna iguana*. New York: Penguin.

Letter Writing 2

Essential Skill

Students will understand the purpose for writing a friendly letter and the characteristics of the content (date, greeting, body, closing).

Materials

• Samples of friendly letters
• Sample letter written on chart paper labeled Characteristics of a Friendly Letter
• Chart titled Letter Writing Word Wall
• Trade books with letter-writing as the central theme (see Suggested Texts)

Procedure

Immersion

1. Begin the immersion with a discussion about the purposes for writing a friendly letter. For example, you can write a friendly letter to give or get information from friends, to give or get family news, to ask or answer questions,

to thank someone for something, or to invite someone for a visit or to attend an event.

2. Together with students, bring in examples of friendly letters to examine and discuss the format, elements, and information presented in the letters.

3. Together with students, categorize the letters into groups according to the purpose of each letter. Refer to the reasons for writing that you previously discussed with students.

4. Read trade books with letter-writing as a central theme (see Suggested Texts).

5. On a chart create a sample containing the characteristics of a friendly letter (date, greeting, body, closing) and hang it in the room for a reference (see Figure 24 and Appendix A for a reproducible friendly letter template).

Collecting

6. Brainstorm a list of potential class- or school-related recipients for a friendly letter and discuss the possible purposes for writing the letter. It's important to use and explain the term *recipient* at this time.

7. Have students generate a personal list of recipients and possible purposes for writing a letter to each person.

Figure 24. Sample Friendly Letter

[Date]
September 6, 2006

[Greeting]
Dear Grandma,

[Body]
How are you? This was a special day. It was my first day in second grade. I have a new teacher. Her name is Mrs. Thomas. I think she is nice. Robert, John, and Timmy are in my class again. Ryan is in a new class. My teacher said we are going to have a family day in my class. Everyone can invite people in their family to come. Can you come? It will be at 11:00 on October, 10, 2006. Please write and tell me if you are coming.

[Closing]
Love,
Kyle

Figure 25. Friendly Letter Idea Chart

Name	Recipient and Purpose for Writing
Carlos	Maria—Telling her that I am going to visit her in Mexico
Sadie	Uncle Bill—Thanking him for sending me a trumpet

8. In their notebooks or folders, ask students to practice writing letters to several of the recipients on their list.

Choosing and Developing an Idea

9. Ask students to pick a recipient for the final draft of their friendly letter. Chart the names of the students, the recipients they choose, and the purpose for writing the letter (see Figure 25).

10. Create a letter-writing word wall and add important words such as *greeting*, *closing*, and *recipient*.

Drafting

11. Review some of the minilessons introduced during the Immersion, such as characteristics of a friendly letter and possible purposes of a friendly letter.

12. Have students draft a friendly letter based on the ideas they charted during the Choosing and Developing an Idea phase.

Revising

13. Model how to reread to check for accuracy. Explain to students that we reread, asking ourselves, "Does this make sense?" and "Will the reader understand my letter?"

14. Have students reread their own letters and letters written by other students, asking themselves these questions.

Editing

15. Ask students to edit for capitalization and punctuation.

16. Ask students to edit for correct spelling of words on the Grade 2 High-Frequency Word List (see Appendix B).

Follow-Up Activities

• Have a class discussion about what circumstances or occasions would prompt students to write a letter. Discuss writing to authors, school personnel, and community helpers, among others. Discuss what the contents of letters to these various recipients might include.

- Set up a letter-writing center and allow students to write letters as frequently as possible.

- Explore how authors use the genre of letter-writing to write picture books. Encourage students to experiment with this genre either individually or with partners.

- Explain that a friendly letter is like a conversation. To understand this concept, have students work with partners, writing friendly letters back and forth to each other.

Assessment

Students will be able to compose a friendly letter that has relevance and demonstrates correct form.

- After the students have drafted their friendly letter, check for correctness of form (should include a date, opening, body, and closing) and clarity of purpose. If necessary, hold a conference with individual students and question the content of their letters. It is acceptable if the student can verbally explain the letter's content, because you are assessing the understanding of the purpose for writing a friendly letter.

Suggested Texts

Ada, A.F. (2005). *Yours truly, Goldilocks*. New York: Simon & Schuster.

Asch, F. (1992). *Dear brother*. New York: Scholastic.

Leedy, L. (1991). *Messages in the mailbox: How to write a letter*. New York: Holiday House.

Teague, M. (2002). *Dear Mrs. La Rue: Letters from obedience school*. New York: Scholastic.

Personal Narrative

Essential Skill

Students will understand that in addition to structure, a personal narrative has a specific focus.

Materials

- Authors' quotes about their views about and experiences with writing and being a writer (see Suggested Texts)

- Heart Map (see Appendix A)

- Two-column chart with columns labeled Idea and Focus
- Trade books that are personal narratives, autobiographies, biographies, and memoirs (see Suggested Texts)

Procedure

Immersion

1. Assemble a basket of outstanding stories based on events from the authors' own lives (see Suggested Texts).

2. Read four or five different stories and discuss with the class where and how they think the authors got their ideas for the stories.

3. Have students collect, read, and share some of their favorite stories. Ask students to infer how the author got the idea for the story based on clues in the text.

4. Read excerpts from biographies and autobiographies of authors' lives. Also, read quotes by authors explaining how they get their ideas for stories (see Suggested Texts). Point out that we can look into authors' lives by reading the blurbs and dedications they write in their books. Explain how many authors use the experiences from their own lives to write their stories. Introduce the idea by saying, "A story from your own life is called a personal narrative."

Collecting

5. Have students generate a list of ideas for stories from their own lives. Each student will keep the list as a reference when he or she needs to generate an idea for a story.

6. Draw a large Heart Map on a chart and section it into parts (see Appendix A). Label each part with an event or a person in your life who is dear to your heart. Explain that each part of the heart is an idea for a story. For example, label one section "my mom," another "trip to Disneyland," and a third section "my new puppy" (see Figure 26).

7. Choose one section of the Heart Map, such as the name of a family member, and say, "When an author has an idea for a story about his family, he has to think about a focus for the story because the author can't write everything about his family in one story. He must narrow his family idea down to a more specific idea." Create a two-column chart with the first column labeled Idea and the second column labeled Focus. Demonstrate how to narrow the ideas on the Heart Map into focused ideas that can then go onto the chart. For

Figure 26. Sectioned Heart Map

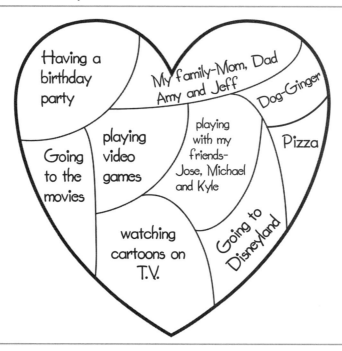

example, if a section of the heart map says "my mom" the focused idea would be "making holiday cookies with my mom" (see Figure 27).

8. Have students draw their own Heart Maps.

9. Ask students to select a section from their Heart Map they might want to write about, and then focus on one special thought relating to that section.

10. Ask students to generate a personal list of focused ideas for stories, using their Heart Maps as a springboard for the ideas.

11. Over several days have students experiment with writing stories, using their list of focused ideas.

Choosing and Developing an Idea

12. Ask students to choose one section of their Heart Map to use for a final draft. Then have them make their selection the focus of a story that they will write about (this can be a part they have already experimented with in their folder or notebook). Do not have students begin writing until the following day.

13. On the following day, return to a touchstone text, which is a text that has become a familiar favorite, and say, "Before an author writes a story, he needs an idea, a focus, and a plan of how the story will go. A personal narrative needs

Figure 27. Idea–Focus Chart

Idea	Focus
My dog	Sprayed by a skunk
My daughter	Spending the day at the mall

to have a beginning that draws the reader in, a middle section that explains what happens, and an end that completes the story." Reread the touchstone text pointing out these main sections. Model how to write a short story related to a section from your Heart Map. Point out the beginning, middle, and end of the story as you write. Then direct students to think about the beginning, the middle, and the end of their own stories, using the idea and focus they chose the preceding day.

Drafting

14. Have students complete their stories with the goal of staying focused and writing within a narrative structure.

15. During conferences, discuss the structure of the piece and what information should be contained in each section.

Revising

16. Using your own story from the modeled lesson, diagram on a chart the structure by marking off and labeling the beginning, the middle, and the end. Explain that the order of events is important because without the structure the story wouldn't make sense to the reader. Have students reread their stories with a partner, checking to make sure their story has a beginning, a middle, and an end.

Editing

17. Have students check spelling, emphasizing that all high-frequency words (see Appendix B) introduced in class must be correct.

18. Assign students an editing buddy to reread and check their stories.

Follow-Up Activities

• Invite students to bring in photographs and artifacts as springboards for generating ideas for personal narratives. Examine photos and ask students to write the story that we can't see, the one that happened before or after the photograph was taken.

• Explain how our senses can trigger ideas for personal narratives. For example, sometimes a certain smell can trigger a favorite memory. Have students bring in a favorite stuffed animal that has a familiar smell or a piece of clothing from a grandparent or parent that has a faint odor from a specific perfume. Ask students to write stories prompted by sensory memorabilia.

• Explain how writers use recurring events to format or structure their stories by relating some special things that happen at these events each time they occur (see Suggested Texts for some possible read-aloud examples). Ask students to experiment with their writing by choosing a specific recurring event, such as a birthday celebration or a yearly dinner at a relative's house, as a focus to write about.

Assessment

Students will demonstrate the ability to select a focused idea and use this idea to write a simple story within a narrative structure.

• Use the finished drafts to assess each student's written work for focus and structure. The pieces should have a beginning, a middle, and an end. They should also center on specific details that describe one event or memory. For example, if a student chose to write about a pet, the narrative should focus on the time the pet got a funny haircut. If the student included other items, such as feeding the pet, he or she would need further demonstration and practice in focusing and sticking to an idea.

Suggested Texts

Personal Narratives
Carle, E. (1994). *My apron.* New York: Penguin.
dePaola, T. (1997). *Tom. New York: Scholastic.*
Johnson, A. (1996). *The leaving morning.* New York: Scholastic.
Martin, B., Jr, & Archambault, J. (1988). *The ghost-eye tree.* New York: Henry Holt.
Rylant, C. (1993). *The relatives came.* New York: Simon & Schuster.
Zolotow, C. (1993). *The moon was the best.* New York: Greenwillow.

Recurring Events
Ada, A.F. (2002). *I love Saturdays y domingos.* New York: Atheneum.
Rylant, C. (1991). *Birthday presents.* New York: Scholastic.

Biography
Polacco, P. (1994). *Firetalking.* New York: Richard C. Owen.
Winter, J. (2005). *Roberto Clemente: Pride of the Pittsburgh Pirates.* New York: Atheneum.

Memoir
Byars, B. (1991). *The moon & I.* New York: Simon & Schuster.

Resources for Authors' Quotes

Fletcher, R. (1996). *A writer's notebook: Unlocking the writer within you.* New York: HarperCollins.

Fletcher, R. (1999). *Live writing: Breathing life into your words.* New York: HarperCollins.

Fletcher, R. (2000). *How writers work: Finding a process that works for you.* New York: HarperCollins.

Grade 2 Reading and Response to Reading Units

Story Structure

Essential Skill

Students will understand that a story has a structure, main idea, and supporting details, and they will understand how to use a graphic organizer to represent these story elements.

Materials

• Story retelling chart (see Appendix A)

• Several familiar texts

Procedure

Modeling

1. Read a familiar story to the class and say, "Sometimes after we read a story we have to retell the story to someone who might not know it. For example, when I confer with you during independent reading I might ask you what the story you're reading is about because I have not read every book in the library. When I do this, I expect you to tell me the important details or the important pieces of information in the beginning, the middle, and the end of the story. Now I'm going to retell the story I just read to you so you will know what parts I thought were the important details." Begin by saying, "When I retell a story I first think about what the story is about or the main idea of the story. Then I think about the important parts in each section—the beginning, middle, and end—that someone who doesn't know the story needs to know in order for the story to make sense." Retell the story in a structured format. Conclude the lesson by stating, "Remember, when we retell a story we follow

the story's structure and we think about the main idea, then we think about a few important parts or details in each section."

2. Repeat reading and retelling new and familiar stories over the next few days.

Guided Reading

3. Read a new story and elicit the main idea and supporting details from the students. Read the story and say, "Today we are going to retell the story together, but we are also going to map out the story on paper. We need to learn how to write our ideas down in case we have to remember details to tell someone else or answer questions or write a report about a story." Next, divide a chart page vertically into three sections. At the top of the page write Title then beneath that write "This story is about...." Then label the remaining sections Beginning, Middle, and End (see Figure 28). Elicit responses from the students about what important parts from the story should go in each section, stressing that only the important details should go in the boxes, and fill in the chart together.

Figure 28. Story Retelling Chart

Title: The Gingerbread Boy This story is mostly about an old man and an old woman who want a son.		
Beginning	Middle	End
The man and woman want a son so they bake a gingerbread boy. The boy jumps out of the oven and runs away.	The old man and the old woman and their friends chase after him. They can't catch him.	The gingerbread boy comes to a river and meets a fox. The fox tricks him into thinking he will take him across the river. The fox eats the gingerbread boy.

4. Repeat this lesson several times, reading different stories and then filling in the chart. This writing may be done interactively as a whole-group shared writing experience on chart paper; the students help to compose the text, then "share the pen" with you during the writing. The goals are to practice using sound–symbol correspondence when writing words, to reinforce knowledge of high-frequency words, and to increase competency in the use of punctuation and capitalization.

Independent Reading

5. After reading independently, ask students to orally retell their books to the entire class or to partners.

6. Students should complete the graphic organizer using the stories they have read during independent reading or guided reading.

Follow-Up Activities

• Read a familiar text with a strong narrative structure, such as *Henny Penny* (Galdone, 1984). Place the students in groups of three and assign each group member the beginning, the middle, or the end of the story. Have each student summarize his or her assigned section of text in one or two sentences and then draw accompanying illustrations. Each group should share with the class.

• Using a familiar story, summarize and write the beginning, middle, and end of the story on sentence strips. Read the strips out of order and ask students to reorder the sentences correctly, placing the strips in a pocket chart.

• Summarize the beginning, the middle, and the end of a story, adding too much detail. Display the summary on an overhead projector and, along with students, cross out the sentences that are not essential to the retelling.

• During writers' workshop ask students to use one of their own stories to complete the story retelling chart. Then they should retell their story to a partner or the class using the graphic organizer as a guide (see Appendix A for a reproducible story retelling chart).

Assessment

Students will understand that a story should be retold by focusing on the most important ideas and details in each section of the story and that a graphic organizer can help to structure the retelling.

• Over several days, read different stories either during read-aloud time or guided reading. In individual conferences, ask students to retell the story by helping you to fill in a graphic organizer. This can be done independently if you determine that the students are able to fill in a graphic organizer.

- Assess the results to determine if students can focus on the most relevant ideas and details in the story and if they are directing you to fill in the organizer in correct sequence.

Suggested Texts

Crews, D. (1998). *Night at the fair.* New York: Greenwillow.
Galdone, P. (1984). *Henny Penny.* Boston: Houghton Mifflin.
Houston, G. (1997). *My great-aunt Arizona.* New York: HarperCollins.
Yolen, J. (1997). *Owl moon.* New York: Penguin.

Story Elements

Essential Skill

Students will understand how to use story elements, including problem and solution, to retell a story both verbally and in writing.

Materials

- Story Map 3 drawn on chart paper (see Appendix A)
- Copies of Story Map 3—one for each student (see Appendix A)
- Copies of Story Frame 3—two for each student (see Appendix A)
- Sticky notes
- Trade books (see Suggested Texts)

Procedure

Modeling

1. Select and read stories in which the story elements are clearly evident, such as in fairy tales and folk tales. Retell these stories in a structured format, emphasizing beginning, middle, and end. After several days of reading stories with strong structures, say to the class, "Sometimes when we retell a story, we need to include more details in order to understand the story better. These additional details are called the story elements, and we are going to think about some of these elements. When we read *The Gingerbread Boy*, the author did not tell us the names of the characters in the story and it still made sense, but in other stories the names of the characters are important to the story. The other story element that could help us to understand a story

better is the setting—or where the story takes place." Retell one or two of the previous stories read but, this time, include the characters' names and the settings. For example, read *The Three Bears* and retell the story without the characters' names or the setting. Say, "This story is about bears and a child who broke into their house." Continue retelling the important parts without using the characters' names or the setting. Retell the story a second time using the names Goldilocks, Mama Bear, Papa Bear, and Baby Bear and also mention that the bears lived in a cottage in the woods. Point out how the names of the characters and recognizing the setting help us to understand the story better.

Guided Reading

2. Read a new story and compare it to a familiar story by asking questions that will lead to a discussion of story elements. Make text-to-text connections between the two stories. For example, ask students, "Does this story remind you of other stories we have read?" "Are the characters similar?" "Is the setting the same?"

3. Introduce the concept of problem–solution. Explain to students that many times in stories the characters are presented with a problem. Then, after several events in the story unfold, the author leads us to a solution for the problem. Read a new story and ask students questions, such as "How is the boy's problem different in this story from the boy's problem in the last story I read?" or "What problem are the three little pigs facing? What events lead the pigs to a solution for their problem?"

4. Read different stories and on different days introduce how to use story maps to chart details such as characters, setting, events, problem and solution (see Appendix A for Story Map 3). Fill in the story map with the class.

5. Over several days read a few different stories and introduce story frames (see Appendix A for Story Frame 3). Fill in a story frame with students. After several scaffolded sessions using a text that all group members have read, ask students to independently fill in a story frame. Have different students share their written response.

Independent Reading

6. Before independent reading, set broad purposes for reading. Say, "While you are reading, think about the main characters and what problems they are having. Think about how they solve their problems."

7. Have students use story maps or story frames to reinforce their knowledge of story elements.

Follow-Up Activities

- Select stories that contain several strong characters, such as *The Three Billy Goats Gruff.* Form small groups, assign students different sections of the text, and have them practice retelling the story in sections focusing on the story elements.

- During independent reading, ask students to put sticky notes in their book when a problem presents itself and when the solution occurs. During conferences, discuss the characters, the problem, and solution in more depth.

- Read a new text without revealing the illustrations. Model using a setting map (see Appendix A) to draw your images of where the action takes place in the story. On subsequent days in small groups read another text. Ask students to draw their images of the setting.

- Use story maps and story frames as responses after read-aloud, guided reading, independent reading sessions, and for homework.

Assessment

Students will be able to rely on story elements to help them construct a verbal or written retelling of a text.

- After reading aloud to the whole class, distribute a story frame (see Appendix A for Story Frame 3) and ask students to fill it in with details from the read-aloud story. Collect the sheets, and during reading conferences ask individual students to retell the story using their sheets as a guide. This also can be done during small-group, guided reading sessions.

Suggested Texts

Blume, J. (1985). *The pain and the great one.* New York: Bantam Dell.

Bottner, B. (1992). *Bootsie Barker bites.* New York: Penguin.

Galdone, P. (1981). *The three billy goats Gruff.* Boston: Houghton Mifflin.

Hoffman, M. (1991). *Amazing Grace.* New York: Dial Books for Young Readers.

Polacco, P. (1998). *My rotten redheaded older brother.* New York: Simon & Schuster.

Waber, B. (1975). *Ira sleeps over.* Boston: Houghton Mifflin.

Change Over Time

Essential Skill

Students will be able to recognize the precipitous events in a story that cause characters to change over time.

Materials

- Several timelines marked Beginning and End drawn on chart paper
- Change Over Time Organizer drawn on chart paper (see Appendix A)
- *Babushka's Doll* (Polacco, 1995) or alternative trade books demonstrating clear character change (see Suggested Texts)
- Sticky notes

Procedure

Modeling

1. In preparation for the lesson, draw a timeline labeled Beginning and End. This will be used to mark the precipitous events that cause a character to change in a story. Assemble the students and read aloud *Babushka's Doll*. Then say, "I was thinking about this book, and I realized in this story the main character changes from the beginning of the story until the end. I think Natasha was very nasty to Basbushka at the beginning of the story, then after she played with the doll Babushka gave her she was nice to Babushka at the end of the story." On the timeline under Beginning and End, write the character traits that describe the character at both points in the story. Continue by saying, "I also noticed that the author of the book doesn't come right out and say the character changes but, rather, marks the changes by certain events that happen in the story. This is called 'showing not telling,' and we have to be good thinkers in order to find the evidence to prove what we think about the character." Then point out the places or events in the story that caused the character to change and mark them on the timeline.

2. Create a chart with several timelines drawn on it. The events from different stories can be written on sticky notes and placed along the timelines. Over several days, read different books; each time point out events that cause the character or characters to change, stressing that the author does not tell us but, rather, shows us what is happening by giving us clues in the story that mark the character's change.

Guided Reading

3. Read a story aloud and then with students map a timeline from the story. Elicit responses from students, describing how the character was at the beginning and end of the story and what events contributed to the change.

4. Using the Change Over Time Organizer together with students fill in the information (see Figure 29 and Appendix A).

Figure 29. Change Over Time Organizer

Title <u>Babushka's Doll</u>   Author Patricia Polacco

Character Natasha

Beginning Natasha is mean to Babushka.

Event Babushka goes out and gives Natasha a doll to play with.

Event The doll comes alive and is mean to Natasha.

Event Grandma comes home and puts the doll back on the shelf.

End Natasha learns to be nice to Babushka.

Independent Reading

5. During independent reading, ask students to complete a Change Over Time Organizer based on the books they are reading.

Follow-Up Activities

• Place students in groups of three. Using multiple copies of a text, assign one student the task of describing how a character was at the beginning of the story, assign one student the task of describing how the character was at the end of the story, and the third student will find evidence in the text to support the change.

• Introduce picture books that demonstrate character change through the illustrations. Have students study different texts either independently or in small groups for visual representation of character change. Then have students orally explain the changes represented in the pictures.

• Using some of the stories previously introduced in these lessons, have students pictorially represent the characters as they change over time.

Assessment

Students will be able to provide textual evidence to support a character's change over time.

- Select a guided reading text that demonstrates a clear character change over time, such as Spring from *Frog and Toad Are Friends* (Lobel, 1970). After reading the story, have students independently complete the Change Over Time Organizer. Assess the responses for accuracy in isolating the events that lead up to the character change.

Suggested Texts

Hoban, R. (1993). *Bread and jam for Frances.* New York: HarperCollins.

Lobel, A. (1970). *Frog and Toad are friends.* New York: HarperCollins.

Polacco, P. (1995). *Babushka's doll.* New York: Simon & Schuster.

Wells, R. (2000). *Noisy Nora.* New York: Penguin.

Characteristics of Genre 4

Essential Skill

Students will understand that each genre has its own characteristics and language.

Materials

- Four-column chart with columns labeled Genre, Title/Example, Characteristics, and Language of the Genre
- Chart titled Favorite Books in Different Genres
- Various trade books in different genres (see Suggested Texts)

Procedure

Modeling

1. Create a four-column chart with columns labeled Genre, Title/Examples, Characteristics, and Language of the Genre. Write the following genres in the Genre column—Poetry, Realistic Fiction, Nonfiction, Fantasy/Fairy Tale, Folk Tale(see Figure 30). Explain to the students that each genre has certain things that make it special. These special qualities are called the characteristics of the genre. Say, "The characteristics of a genre allow us to recognize what genre we are reading. Knowing certain things about a genre can help us clear up any confusions we may have had while we read. Also learning these characteristics can help us write in some of these genres."

2. During the next several weeks read examples of each genre. Be explicit about which genre is being read and point out specific examples of characteristics

Figure 30. Characteristics of Genre Chart

Genre	Title/Example	Characteristics	Language of the Genre
Folk Tales	Anansi the Spider stories	Talking animals	"Long ago..." "In the days of..."
Realistic Fiction	*Jamaica Tag-Along* (Havill, 1989)	Familiar people Realistic settings	Familiar names Familiar setting descriptions
Fantasy/Fairy Tale	*The Gingerbread Baby* (Brett, 1999)	Magical things	"Once upon a time..."
Nonfiction	*Bridges Are to Cross* (Sturges, 1998)	Captions Drawings Labels	Depends on the topic Index Glossary
Poetry	*Creatures of the Earth, Sea, and Sky* (Heard, 1997)	White space Line breaks	Interesting words Sound words

of the genre. For instance, if you read fairy tales point out that one of the characteristics of that genre is that magical things happen.

3. Brainstorm with the class about what should be written on the chart for each text read. After repeated discussions and several chart entries in each column, post the chart for reference.

4. Create another chart titled Favorite Books in Different Genres. Fill this one in collaboratively with students, adding book titles from read-aloud, guided reading, or independent reading.

Guided Reading

5. Select guided reading books that are representative of the various genres you have previously introduced. Before reading a particular book, introduce the genre of the selection, then ask students for examples of characteristics of the genre they can expect to find in the book. After reading have students validate their predictions by returning to the text and pointing out the characteristics they noticed while reading. Also ask them to look for any new characteristics that can be added to the Characteristics of Genre chart previously created.

Independent Reading

6. For a period of time focus the independent reading specifically around certain genres. For example, for several days have everyone reading poetry or

nonfiction at their appropriate level. After everyone has read from the different genres, ask students to write recommendations for their favorite books in the different genres. Create a recommendation board that has a column for each of the genres, and post students' recommendations under each appropriate genre.

Follow-Up Activities

• Continue to post entries on the chart throughout the year.

• Have students experiment by writing in different genres during writers' workshop. An original piece can be written in a certain genre or an old piece can be rewritten in a new genre. Encourage students to examine the characteristics and language of a genre when they are writing or rewriting.

• Create and ask students to use a grade 2 reading log (see Appendix B) to track their independent reading. Include designation of genre, title, and author.

• Several times during the year, ask students to graph their reading logs by genre. In this way they can set reading goals around which genres they need to read more of.

Assessment

Students will demonstrate recognition of various genres by the characteristics and language of the genre.

• When reading aloud throughout the year, ask students genre-related questions. For example, when reading stop and say, "This story is sounding like other stories we have read. What genre would you say it belongs to? How do you know?" Expect students to name at least two characteristics of a genre.

• When students write in certain genres, assess their work by how well they have included characteristics of the genre in their pieces. For example, if students are writing nonfiction the piece should be fact based and there should be evidence of an attempt to inform or persuade.

Suggested Texts

Poetry

Heard, G. (1997). *Creatures of the earth, sea, and sky.* Honesdale, PA: Boyds Mills Press.

Worth, V. (1996). *All the small poems and fourteen more.* New York: Farrar, Straus and Giroux.

Nonfiction

Davies, N. (2005). *One tiny turtle.* Cambridge, MA: Candlewick.

Gibbons, G. (2000). *My baseball book.* New York: HarperCollins.

Sturges, P. (1998). *Bridges are to cross.* New York: Penguin.

Fantasy/Fairy Tale

Brett, J. (1999). *Gingerbread baby.* New York: Putnam.

Garland, M. (2005). *Miss Smith's incredible storybook.* New York: Penguin.

Sendak, M. (1991). *Where the wild things are.* New York: HarperCollins.

Realistic Fiction

Havill, J. (1989). *Jamaica tag-along.* Boston: Houghton Mifflin.

Keats, E.J. (1976). *The snowy day.* New York: Penguin.

Williams, V.B. (1984). *A chair for my mother.* New York: HarperCollins.

Folk Tales

Arkhurst, J.C., & Pinkney, J. (1992). *The adventures of spider: West African folktales.* New York: Holiday House.

Brett, J. (1989). *The mitten.* New York: HarperCollins.

dePaola, T. (1997). *Jamie O'Rourke and the big potato.* New York: Penguin.

Compare/Contrast/Conclude

Essential Skill

Students will be able to compare elements from more than one text and then use a graphic organizer to support an opinion based on evidence found in the texts.

Materials

• T-chart drawn on chart paper

• Several pairs of trade books with similar themes (see Suggested Texts)

• Articles from student newsmagazines

Procedure

Modeling

1. Select and read two texts with similarities in characters, plot, and main idea, such as *Big Al* (Clements, 1997) and *Babushka's Doll* by (Polacco, 1995). Formulate an opinion about the similarities between the two books and say, "I think the authors of both of these books want us to think that we need to treat each other kindly. This is my opinion about the books' main ideas or what the

authors want us to learn from their books. An opinion is an idea we have in our heads that we get from putting pieces of information together about a topic. An opinion is not just what we think, it needs information to back it up or support it. I think about an opinion like it is a table—the top of the table is our opinion or idea about something. The legs of the table are the facts that support our opinion or hold it up. If I want to support my opinion about what the authors are telling us in these two books, I need to go back into the story to find the facts that support my opinion." Model how to look through the two books to find places where there is evidence to support your opinion. (Note: This can be stated or inferred evidence, but if it is inferred it should be explained.)

2. Return to the two stories and model how to put the information into a T-chart, with the opinion at the top and supporting details listed in each column (see Figure 31).

Guided Reading

3. Read two short pieces and form an opinion about the similarities or differences in both of the stories. Write the opinion on the top of the T-chart. Have the students work in small groups to find evidence in the text to support the opinion. The groups will come together to share and record the evidence on the T-chart. Repeat this activity several times.

4. Read two short texts with students. After the readings give each student an individual response sheet (a T-chart with an opinion stated at the top, drawn from the two stories). Ask students to fill in the necessary evidence from the stories to prove the opinion

Independent Reading

5. Select multiple copies of several short texts or articles. Have each student independently read two texts. Place the students in groups of four and ask each

Figure 31. Opinion With Supporting Details T-Chart

It is important to be nice to each other.	
Big Al (Clements, 1997)	*Babushka's Doll* (Polacco, 1995)
1. The fish made fun of Big Al because he was ugly. 2. The fish were in danger. 3. Big Al was the only fish who could help. 4. He helped even though they had been mean to him. 5. They learned to be nice.	1. The little girl was mean to her grandmother. 2. The doll was mean to the little girl. 3. She learned a lesson from the doll. 4. She learned to be nice.

group to formulate a common opinion about the two texts. Then ask one student to be the recorder, two to gather the evidence, and one to post the information on the T-chart. Give each group their own piece of chart paper with the opinion written on the top. (For example, a group opinion could state, "We enjoyed these books because they were both very scary." Group members would then find and record evidence of scary parts in the two texts.)

Follow-Up Activities

• Repeat the lessons using expository texts such as articles from student news-magazines or sections of text from nonfiction books.

• Repeat the lessons using both narrative and expository texts. For example, chose an expository text about spiders and one of the Anansi the Spider folk tales. Formulate an opinion such as "Spiders are smart and tricky." Ask students to find information in both texts to support the opinion.

• Have students do a comparison on a T-chart using information found in both narrative and expository texts. For example, ask students to find out how real spiders get food and how Anansi the Spider gets food. Set up the T-chart with the question How Do Spiders Get Food? across the top. Under the left column write Real Spiders and under the right column write Anansi the Spider. Have students fill in the appropriate information from each book.

Assessment

Students will be able to form an opinion and back up their opinion with details from the story.

• Ask students to individually complete a T-chart as a response to two stories read during guided reading. Along with students, discuss and formulate an opinion concerning a possible lesson learned from the two texts. Have students find supporting evidence for the opinion in both texts to fill in the T-chart. Assess students' work based on relevance of material selected to support the opinion.

Suggested Texts

Arkhurst, J.C., & Pinkney, J. (1992). *The adventures of spider: West African folk tales.* New York: Holiday House.

Clements, A. (1997). *Big Al.* New York: Simon & Schuster.

Fitch, S. (2001). *No two snowflakes.* Victoria, BC: Orca Book.

Polacco, P. (1995). *Babushka's doll.* New York: Simon & Schuster.

Tarpley, N.A. (2001). *I love my hair!* Boston: Little, Brown.

Wing, N. (1996). *Jalapeño bagels.* New York: Simon & Schuster.

Woodson, J. (2001). *The other side.* New York: Penguin.

Essential Skill

Students will be able to recognize and retell a story around the main idea with supporting details.

Materials

• Several trade books that are new to students (see Suggested Texts)
• Large story retelling chart drawn on chart paper (see Appendix A)

Procedure

Modeling

1. Select and read a new book. At the conclusion say, "Sometimes we will need to tell a story to someone who doesn't know the story we are reading. This can happen when I ask you about what you are reading during independent reading, when you read your 'just-right' book. I do not know all of the stories in all of the baskets, so if I want to make sure you understand what you are reading, I will ask you to tell me what the story is about. A friend might also ask you what a story is about because they might be interested in reading the same story." Then explain how to retell a story using the main idea as a starting point and, filling in the important details and pieces of information from the beginning, the middle, and the end of the story, say, "We retell a story around the main idea and give details about the beginning, middle, and end so that the story makes sense to the listener."

2. Tell students that retelling helps someone know what the story is mostly about. Then read a new story, but this time retell the story using a structured format such as "This story is about.... In the beginning...in the middle...and at the end...."

Guided Reading

3. Read a story to the class and then elicit the main idea and supporting details from the students. Ask different students to retell the story using a structured format.

4. Repeat this lesson using texts from different genres.

5. Introduce how to use a story retelling chart for support when writing a brief summary (see Figure 32 and Appendix A). Refer back to previous lessons about story structure and story elements when writing the summary. Write

Figure 32. Book Summary Based on Story Retelling Chart

Title: *Danny and the Dinosaur*

Main Idea: Danny has adventures with a dinosaur that comes to life

Beginning	Middle	End
Danny went to the museum and met a dinosaur that came to life.	Danny and the dinosaur left the museum and visited a lot of different places and had a lot of fun.	Danny wanted the dinosaur to go home with him, but it had to return to the museum.

The story is about a little boy named Danny who has adventures with a dinosaur that comes to life. Danny went to a museum and met a dinosaur that came to life. The dinosaur left the museum with Danny, and they visited a lot of places. They had a lot of fun! Danny wanted the dinosaur to go home with him. The dinosaur had to go back to the museum.

the summary using the story retelling chart for support and include some story elements as details.

Independent Reading

6. During shared reading time ask different students to orally retell their independent reading books to partners or the whole group. Students can retell the story using a story web as a guide.

Follow-Up Activities

• Read and retell a new story using a structured format. Then fill in a story web (see Appendix A) focusing on the main idea and supporting details in each part of the story.

• Introduce book talks. Model how to give a book talk from a read-aloud book. Explain that the book talk should include the title, the main idea, a few interesting details about the story, and whether or not you enjoyed the book. Repeat the activity several times throughout the year, asking students to give a book talk either in small groups or to the whole class.

Assessment

Students will demonstrate the ability to read and explain a story's main idea by supplying details to support their explanation.

• During independent reading conferences, after a student has completed a book ask about the book's main idea. Then ask the student to supply some details from the story to support his or her thinking.

Suggested Texts

Abercrombie, B. (1995). *Charlie Anderson.* New York: Simon & Schuster.

Hoff, S. (1992). *Danny and the dinosaur.* New York: HarperCollins.

Sharp, N.L. (1997). *Today I'm going fishing with my dad.* Honesdale, PA: Boyds Mills Press.

Zolotow, C. (1990). *I like to be little.* New York: HarperCollins.

CHAPTER 5

Grade 3: Building on a Solid Foundation

G rade 3 is a crucial year. According to NCLB legislation, all students will have to demonstrate mastery of standards-based curriculum through state-mandated assessments near the end of grade 3. When students have been taught the necessary foundational skills in kindergarten and grades 1 and 2, however, the grade 3 teacher does not have the added pressure of fully preparing students for state-mandated assessments in the few short months prior to the examinations. Instead, when a school follows a consistent cyclical language arts curriculum, grade 3 teachers can immediately begin to prepare students in the reading and writing skills necessary to meet the demands required by state standards and assessments—and, more importantly, this preparation does not have to overtake all language arts instruction prior to the state-mandated assessments. This means that teachers can meet the bigger and more important goal: to ensure students have the well-rounded instruction that leads to solid foundational skills necessary to leading literate lives.

Building on the literacy curriculum outlined in the previous chapters, student writers in grade 3 will learn that purpose drives the form of writing, and they'll learn to use their background knowledge to focus and structure their writing for an intended audience. Grade 3 students will learn to add interesting details and events aimed at catching and sustaining a reader's attention.

The suggested minilessons that are part of the grade 3 writing units should take approximately 20 minutes each. Writing sessions in which students choose, develop, and draft their story ideas should start at about 25 minutes but should extend to around 35–40 minutes later in the year; revising and editing should also take about 25 minutes in the beginning of the year but extend as needed later in the year.

Grade 3 students will be reading and responding by writing story summaries, completing story maps and story webs, and engaging in conversations around text elements in order to demonstrate deeper understanding of text. They will be asked to demonstrate in both oral and written form the ability to recognize the main idea of a story and then support their thinking with evidence from the text. They will read extensively in different genres both individually and as a group, and they will be asked to identify a genre by its characteristics. Grade 3 readers will also be asked to support an opinion or answer a question by collecting information from multiple texts on the same topic.

The whole-class minilessons that are part of the reading units should take approximately 20 minutes. Guided reading should go about 20 minutes per group throughout the year, but independent reading should start at around 15 minutes at the beginning of the year and extend to 25–30 minutes as reading stamina increases.

Students who were introduced to the units of study that are part of the continuum in kindergarten and grades 1 and 2 should enter grade 3 as more confident learners. They should demonstrate greater mastery of the skills demanded at this level because of their previous background knowledge and experience with an essential literacy skills curriculum. This continuum of instruction should help teachers in all grades feel that they have shared ownership in the preparation of students who will have to meet the demands of standards-based learning; state-mandated assessments; and, most importantly, the ever-changing literacy world that they live in.

Grade 3 Writing Units

Functional Writing

Essential Skill

Students will understand that the purpose of the writing drives the structure.

Materials

- Samples of functional writing (postcards, invitations, advertisements, recipes)
- Various types of writing paper and blank notecards
- Chart paper
- Trade books focused on functional writing—primarily postcard writing (see Suggested Texts)

Procedure

Immersion

1. Together with students collect samples of functional writing, focusing specifically on postcards, invitations, advertisements, and recipes.

2. Explain that writers must decide on the purpose of their writing and their audience before they select a structure or format in which to craft their writing.

3. Together with students examine the features of the different samples they have collected. Discuss the difference between a postcard and a letter. Point out, too, that an advertisement must capture the audience's attention quickly and hold their interest

4. Together with students create a chart with a template for each type of writing. This chart will remain up all year as a reference.

5. Read trade books focusing on functional writing and point out features that are unique to each type.

Collecting

6. Collectively decide on a purpose for writing, then choose the format that would best meet the purpose and compose a piece with the class. For example, ask a "celebrity reader" to come to the classroom by writing an invitation to the vice principal.

7. Students can try out several of these formats in their writer's notebooks or folders.

Choosing and Developing an Idea

8. Ask students to select a piece from their writer's notebook for their final draft. Have students try out two formats to decide which one they will use for their piece. They may consult with partners.

Drafting

9. Have students choose the paper and format they want to use for their final drafts and then begin writing.

Revising

10. Using a postcard format write about a recent event. Include unnecessary information when writing the events. Before beginning the revision explain that we do not always need to add information when we revise; sometimes we need to eliminate unnecessary information. Revise the writing, focusing on eliminating the unnecessary information (see Figure 33).

11. Ask students to reread their drafts. Tell them to keep the information that centers on the main focus of their pieces and eliminate unnecessary information.

Editing

12. Reinforce the idea that writing has to be correct once it goes out into the world. Ask students to circle any words they think are misspelled. During conferences help them to correct any words that have been overlooked.

Figure 33. Eliminating Unnecessary Postcard Text

June 14, 2003

Dear Jimmy,
The Ghost Coaster was great. It was a roller coaster in the dark. I wasn't too scared but other people were screaming. ~~Did you get our new classes from school yet? I hope we are in the same class.~~ Tomorrow we are going to Great Adventure in New Jersey.
I think the Ghost Coaster will be hard to beat.

Your friend,
Ted

Jimmy Clark

14 Pear St.

Towson, Maryland 12345

13. Create a Grade 3 Editing Checklist (see Appendix B) for students to keep in their writer's notebooks.

14. Assign editing partners. Have them check the Grade 3 High-Frequency Word List (see Appendix B) for correct spelling.

Follow-Up Activity

• Introduce the idea that a writer can use the structures the class has been examining, such as postcards and recipes, to relay other information to a reader. These formats can also be used to write personal narratives. Over several days read trade books demonstrating how these formats can be used as structures for writing in different genres. For example, an author can write about a trip he or she has taken by telling the story using postcards as the format or structure (as in *Stringbean's Trip to the Shining Sea* [Williams, 1999]) or write a story about friendship using a recipe format. Have students try out some of these structures in their writer's notebook using old pieces or writing new ones.

Assessment

Students will demonstrate the ability to correctly write a postcard, invitation, or advertisement that includes focused, relevant details that inform the reader.

• After students write their final draft, compare the results with the initial draft. Check the finished results for correctness of format and relevance of information.

Suggested Texts

Leedy, L. (1996). *Postcards from Pluto: A tour of the solar system*. New York: Holiday House.
Radca, C., & Radca, J. (2003). *Global girl (Betty Spaghetty)*. New York: Random House.
Williams, V.B. (1999). *Stringbean's trip to the shining sea*. New York: HarperCollins.

Essential Skill

Students will become familiar with the purpose for each component in the structure of a friendly letter and understand that there is variety within each component.

Materials

- Samples of friendly letters (original and in texts)
- Various types of writing paper
- Transparency or chart of two letters with same content but different presentation
- Trade books focused on letter writing (see Suggested Texts)

Procedure

Immersion

1. Collect samples of friendly letters from both students and books.

2. Examine the components and discuss the purpose for each part of the structure—the opening or salutation starts the conversation with the reader, the body contains the information the reader will receive, and the closing signals the end of the letter.

3. Examine the letters again. Discuss and then chart possible recipients for a friendly letter and reasons for writing to them.

Collecting

4. Compose a prompt that will lead students to write a friendly letter informing the reader about themselves. For example,

> Write a letter to your teacher telling him or her some surprising things about yourself. Be sure to include
>
> 1. An opening for your letter
> 2. Some interesting things about yourself
> 3. A closing for your letter

5. Have students reread the entries in their writer's notebooks looking for inspiration—something they have written that may spark a reason to write a letter.

6. Ask students to try out different openings and closings.

Choosing and Developing an Idea

7. Read several trade books that contain a friendly letter (see Suggested Texts) and discuss how the author made the letter interesting. For example, discuss word choice, use of punctuation, or formats of print such as boldface lettering or italics for emphasis.

8. Ask students to choose a recipient for a friendly letter and then have them list some information they would like to include in their letter.

Drafting

9. Have students write their letters focusing on the information they want to include and one or two techniques to provoke interest.

Revising

10. Present two samples of previously written letters with the same content—but with some differences in word choice, punctuation, formats of print, openings, or closings (see Figure 34). Discuss which letter is more interesting to read and why. Make the point that sometimes a small change, such as choosing a catchy closing, can make a letter more interesting.

Figure 34. Samples of Two Friendly Letters

June 14, 2003,

Dear Alice,

Today I had a really good time. I went to the Great Escape amusement park in Lake George, New York. I went on a really fast roller coaster. It went up very high. The people were screaming and saying, "Get me off of here." I have to admit I was a little scared myself. Tomorrow I am going to Great Adventure in New Jersey. I love roller coasters. I hear they have some really good ones. I will write soon and let you know.

Your friend,

Bobby

June 14, 2003

Hi there!!

Today I had a really cool time. I went to the Great Escape amusement park in Lake George, New York. I went on a superfast roller coaster. It zoomed up to the top at superfast speed. The people were screaming, "GET ME OFF OF HERE!!!" I have to admit I was scared myself. Tomorrow I am going to Great Adventure in New Jersey. I love, love, love roller coasters. I hear they have some really cool ones there. I will write soon and let you know.

Bye for now,

Bobby

11. Ask students to reread their letters and to try making simple changes in wording, punctuation, closing, and so on.

Editing

12. Edit the letters using an editing checklist (see Appendix B) or partners.

13. Have students check high-frequency words for accuracy (see Appendix B).

Follow-Up Activities

- Read trade books that use a letter-writing format to tell a story (see Suggested Texts). Explain that sometimes writers use this structure to tell "life" stories (similar to the examples in the functional writing unit).

- Have students reread their notebooks for old entries that can serve as inspirations for experimenting with a letter-writing format to tell a story. Ask students to use the information in their notebook entry to write a story in letter format.

- Letter writing should be used throughout the year for different purposes. It can serve as an alternative format for writing a report, inviting visitors to a class function, or getting information from outside sources.

Assessment

Students will demonstrate the ability to compose and write a friendly letter.

- After students finish revising and editing their letters, compare the final drafts with the initial drafts. Check for correctness in format, focus, and relevance of information. Check the letter against a letter-writing rubric (see Appendix B).

Suggested Texts

Cherry, L. (1999). *The armadillo from Amarillo*. San Diego, CA: Harcourt.
Cleary, B. (2000). *Dear Mr. Henshaw*. New York: HarperCollins.
George, J.C. (1995). *Dear Rebecca, winter is here*. New York: HarperCollins.
Gray, L.M. (2000). *Dear Willie Rudd*. New York: Aladdin.
Nolen, J. (2005). *Plantzilla*. San Diego, CA: Harcourt.

Personal Narrative 3

Essential Skill

Students will understand that a personal narrative has a focus, a structure, and details to enhance understanding and interest.

Materials

- Chart titled Characteristics of Personal Narrative
- Story web (see Appendix A)
- Three-column chart with columns labeled Name, Main Idea, and Focus
- Trade books written as personal narratives (see Suggested Texts)

Procedure

Immersion

1. Begin the study by reminding students that personal narrative is a story written about something that has happened in the writer's life. Continue to explain that when a personal narrative is written it has a structure. It is written with a beginning, a middle, and an end. This structure allows the story to make sense to the reader.

2. Read several trade books that are written as personal narratives (see Suggested Texts).

3. After an initial reading, examine several of the personal narratives with the students. Identify the focus of the story and how the narrative was enhanced by the use of details. Also notice how a personal narrative is generally written in the first person.

4. Along with students create a chart titled Characteristics of Personal Narrative to leave up as a reference. Include the identifying features concerning the structure, as well as other observations made by students during the read-alouds.

5. Introduce writing a personal narrative within a narrative structure. Begin by drawing a labeled story web on a chart for planning the writing (see Appendix A). Model how to create the outline for a personal narrative by placing the major points of the beginning, middle, and end of the story into the labeled story web. Point out that the center cell should contain the main focus of the story (for instance, going to a baseball game with your dad) along with the title, but mention that the title can be decided on either before the story is written or after it is completed.

6. Write the narrative as a model for students using the web as a guide.

Collecting

7. Discuss how sometimes we find out about our own lives from others. For example, we generally don't remember our earliest birthday parties. Suggest

that students interview family and friends as sources for information about parts of their lives that are unfamiliar to them.

8. Ask students to begin writing personal narratives in their writer's notebooks. Allow them to experiment with different ideas.

Choosing and Developing an Idea

9. Ask students to reread their writer's notebooks for an idea to use as a draft.

10. Create a three-column chart with columns labeled Name, Main Idea, and Focus (see Figure 35). List the names of the students and their Main Ideas. Leave the last column blank.

11. Model how to consider a topic and focus on one section of the story. For example, if going fishing with Dad is the main idea, then catching a catfish or falling out of the boat would be the focus.

12. After students have selected a focus, write it on the chart. Next, have students create a story web.

13. Have students plan several different personal narratives using a story web.

Drafting

14. Have students write their personal narratives using one of the story webs as a guide.

15. Confer with students either individually or in small groups to make sure the narrative stays focused and that they don't begin to add a lot of extraneous information to the piece.

Revising

16. Using the story web introduced during the Immersion phase of the unit, ask students to look over the details they originally planned when they created the story web. Ask them to try adding one or two more details about their focused topic to each section of their draft.

Editing

17. Students should edit their writing using the Grade 3 Editing Checklist (see Appendix B).

18. Students can confer with editing partners.

Figure 35. Personal Narrative Idea Chart

Name	Big Idea	Focus
Joe	Trip to Disney World	Going on Space Mountain
Sadie	My Birthday Party	Getting my nails done

19. Students should check the Grade 3 High-Frequency Word List for accuracy (see Appendix B).

Follow-Up Activities

• Discuss and model techniques such as adding dialogue to give voice and personality to a piece.

• During the editing phase, discuss how to properly use quotation marks to indicate where speech begins and ends.

• Focus on word choice by making lists of new and interesting words to replace old and tired words. For example, replace *said* with *replied* or *whispered*.

Assessment

Students will be able to plan and write a personal narrative with appropriate structure, focus, and details. Check the writing against a personal narrative rubric (see Appendix B).

• After completion of the final drafts, check that the students' personal narratives are within a narrative structure and that they included some interesting details.

• Check for focus and the elimination of excessive or repetitive content.

Suggested Texts

Beard, D.B. (2003). *Twister*. New York: Farrar, Straus and Giroux.

Hest, A. (1997). *Jamaica Louise James*. Cambridge, MA: Candlewick.

Long, M. (2003). *How I became a pirate*. San Diego, CA: Harcourt.

Paulsen, G. (2001). *Canoe days*. New York: Random House.

Sharp, N.L. (1997). *Today I'm going fishing with my dad*. Honesdale, PA: Boyds Mills Press.

Grade 3 Reading and Response to Reading Units

Story Structure

Essential Skill

Students will understand that using a graphic organizer to summarize a story according to its structure (emphasizing the main idea and supporting details in each section) will help them to construct a written response to reading that will make sense.

Materials

• Story web (see Appendix A) recreated on a chart
• Individual story webs (see Appendix A)—one for each student
• Several familiar stories (see Suggested Texts)

Procedure

Modeling

1. Read a familiar story from beginning to end. Explain to students that a story has a structure (a beginning, a middle, and an end) and this structure helps the story to make sense. Continue explaining that often we have to tell or write about a story for a book talk, a book recommendation, or a book summary. Tell students that when we do this we don't want to tell the whole story; instead we focus on the important parts in each section. Tell them that we can use a story web to organize our ideas before we have to write or tell about a story. Create a story web (see Appendix A) using a familiar story. Model how to sift through each section to pull out the important information and the details that support this information. For example, ask, "What is the important information I need to know in order to tell this story to someone who doesn't know it? What details from the story support the major ideas?" Write the information on the story web.

2. Repeat the above lesson using another familiar story. This time model how to write a book summary using information from the story web (see Figure 36).

Guided Reading

3. Read a new story and complete a story web with input from the students. Then ask students to write their own summaries based on the web.

Independent Reading

4. Students should choose a book to read on their own and then complete a story web and write their own book summaries.

5. Throughout the year, have students use a story web to plan and write summaries of their independent reading books.

Follow-Up Activities

• Demonstrate to students how to give a book talk, using the story web as a guide. Ask them to give book talks to partners or in small groups.

Figure 36. Book Summary Based on Story Web

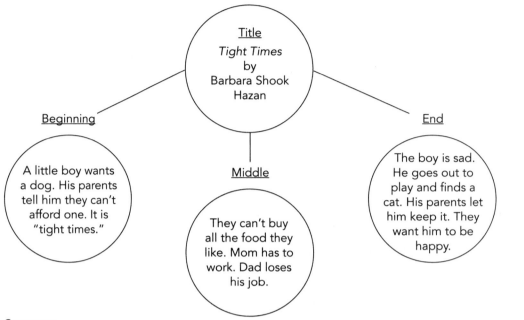

Book Summary

Title: *Tight Times*

Author: Barbara Shook Hazen

This story is about a little boy who wants a dog, but his parents tell him he can't have one because of "tight times." His dad explains that "tight times" are when everything is going up. His dad explains that they have to change some things they are used to because of "tight times." They can't eat everything they like and mom has to work. Later in the story the dad loses his job and everyone is sad. The little boy goes outside to play and finds a cat. He wonders if his parents will let him keep it. The parents decide to let him keep it, because even though it is "tight times" they want him to be happy. The little boy decides to name the cat Dog.

- Read a new story to the class and complete a story web, using input from the students to fill in the cells. Then write a book recommendation, using input from the students (see Figure 37).
- Create a class recommendation board on which students can post recommendations from their independent reading selections. These recommendations should be centered on the story structure.
- Students can examine story summaries on the book jackets of published books and then create a story web, thinking about how the author would have outlined the information included in the summary.
- Students can examine books that have different story structures. For example, books can have a circular structure—they begin and end in the same place

Figure 37. Book Recommendation

Recommended by: Steven Smith

Title and author of the book: <u>Enemy Pie</u> by Derek Munson

Genre: Fiction

Short summary of the book (4–5 sentences): A new boy moves into the neighborhood and he is not nice to one of the kids who lives there. The boy asks his Dad for help to get rid of the new kid. The Dad tells him he will bake him an enemy pie and that will solve the problem. He also says that one of the secret ingredients is that he has to spend a day with his enemy. The boy does as his dad says and at the end of the day when the pie is ready to eat the two boys have become friends.

What is your opinion of the book? Would you recommend the book, or not? Why?
I recommend this book because it is funny and it has a surprise ending.

(such as *The Relatives Came* [Rylant, 1993]), a snapshot structure—all the events take place on the same day or moment in time (such as *Some Birthday!* [Polacco, 1993]), or a clothesline structure—a series of events that are tied together by an object or occurrence (such as *The Keeping Quilt* [Polacco, 2001]).

• During writers' workshop students can use a story web to summarize life events, such as dinner at grandma's house or a family trip, and write a story using the story web as an outline.

Assessment

Students will be able to summarize a book in written form using a story web to construct a response that contains a main idea and supporting details.

• Read a story to the class. Students should be able to complete a story web based on the story and then write an accurate summary of the story.

Suggested Texts

Brinckloe, J. (1986). *Fireflies!* New York: Simon & Schuster.
Hazen, B.S. (1983). *Tight times.* New York: Penguin.

Polacco, P. (1993). *Some birthday!* New York: Simon & Schuster.
Polacco, P. (2001). *The keeping quilt.* New York: Simon & Schuster.
Rylant, C. (1993). *The relatives came.* New York: Simon & Schuster.
Rylant, C. (2002). *Tulip sees America.* New York: Scholastic.
Williams, V.B. (1984). *A chair for my mother.* New York: HarperCollins.
Yolen, J. (1997). *Owl moon.* New York: Penguin.

Story Elements

Essential Skill

Students will understand how to formulate an extended written response using story elements to construct meaning.

Materials

• Three-column chart with columns labeled Characters, Setting, and Plot
• Several character webs created on chart paper (see Appendix A)
• Individual character webs or story maps—one for each student
• Setting map drawn on chart paper (see Appendix A)
• Sticky notes
• Several familiar and new trade books

Procedure

Modeling

1. Begin this lesson by explaining that whenever an author decides to write a story, she usually has a plan in her mind of how the story will go. The author knows the story will have a beginning, a middle, and an end that will allow the story to make sense. The author also knows she will have to include certain story elements that will help to make the story interesting. These story elements usually include characters, setting, plot, and some kind of character change. Explain that the plot is the pattern of events in a narrative that moves the story along. Read a familiar story, discussing what story elements the author needed to think about in order to write the story and make it interesting. Create a three-column chart with the first column labeled Characters, the second column labeled Setting, and the third column labeled Plot. With student input begin to fill in the chart (see Figure 38).

2. Return to the chart constructed the previous day. Say, "We can use our knowledge of story elements to help us respond to specific questions about a story

and to get a better understanding of the story." Create a question such as "What is this story mostly about?" Then model how thinking about the story elements will help to formulate a good written response to the story. Write on chart paper a response beginning with "This story is mostly about..." and then include relevant details based on the story (see Figure 39). Keep this response displayed for future reference.

Guided Reading

3. Read another familiar story to the class and discuss the story's elements. Together with students use the story elements to write a response to the question "What is this story mostly about?"

4. Reread a familiar text paying particular attention to the characters. After completing the story, introduce a character web to the class (see Appendix A). Complete the character web using the main character in the story. Along with students, complete another character web using a secondary character or characters from a different story.

Figure 38. Story Elements Chart

Title: *Shortcut*
Author: Donald Crews

Characters	Setting	Plot
Seven children	Railroad tracks	The children decide to take a shortcut home along the railroad tracks.
		They look and listen to make sure a train is not coming.
		It seems OK so they start walking along the tracks.
		They hear a train coming.
		They get scared.
		They jump off the tracks.
		They never take the shortcut again.

Figure 39. Response to Story, Based on Story Elements Chart

What is the story *Shortcut* by Donald Crews mostly about?

The story *Shortcut* by Donald Crews is mostly about seven children who decide to take a shortcut home. They are supposed to take the road home, but they decide to walk along the railroad tracks instead. They are a little scared, but they look and listen to make sure a train is not coming. They start walking along the tracks and then they hear a train whistle. They knew the train was coming closer because the whistle kept getting louder. They had to jump off the tracks onto a steep slope. The train passed and they were all fine, but they were very scared. They never took the shortcut again.

Figure 40. Chart of Plot Using Sticky Notes

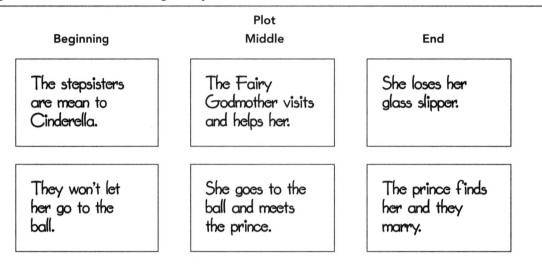

Plot

| Beginning | Middle | End |

The stepsisters are mean to Cinderella.

The Fairy Godmother visits and helps her.

She loses her glass slipper.

They won't let her go to the ball.

She goes to the ball and meets the prince.

The prince finds her and they marry.

5. Read a new story in which the setting is vividly laid out in the story. At the completion of the story create a setting map (see Appendix A) based on the description of the setting outlined in the text.

6. Reread the story used in the first minilesson, but this time focus on explaining the plot as the series of events that occur in the beginning, middle, and end of the story that lead to the resolution or change in the story. Write the events in each part of the story on sticky notes and place the sticky notes in the correct order (see Figure 40). Return to the story, pointing out the transitions between parts of the story or how the author uses time to move the plot along; ask questions such as, "How much time has passed?" and "How do we know?"

Independent Reading

7. After a guided reading session ask students to independently complete a character web or story map (see Appendix A) and write a story summary about the character from the guided reading text.

8. Ask students to complete a character web or story map on their own, based on their independent reading book.

Follow-Up Activities

• Teach students how to give a book talk using the story elements as a framework for the talk.

- Create a class recommendation board for the students to post recommendations from their independent reading selections. These recommendations should be centered on the story elements.
- Students will pick a favorite character, a character they dislike, or one they connect with and use a character map for planning. Then they will write a response explaining why they chose this character.
- Students can draw and share their images of a character or setting and then explain what prompted the visualization.
- During writers' workshop, students can write a short story emphasizing one of the story elements. For example, students can return to a previously written piece and vividly describe the setting or embellish a character by adding more traits.

Assessment

Students will demonstrate writing a response to reading using the story elements as a guide to construct meaning.

- Students will choose an independent reading book. Using a story map to outline the characters, setting, and plot of the story, they will write a simple story summary.

Suggested Texts

Blos, J.W. (1990). *Old Henry.* New York: HarperCollins.
Creech, S. (2003). *A fine, fine school.* New York: HarperCollins.
Crews, D. (1996). *Shortcut.* New York: HarperCollins.
Naylor, P.R. (1994). *The king of the playground.* New York: Simon & Schuster.
Oppenheim, S.L. (2005). *Yanni rubbish.* Honesdale, PA: Boyds Mills Press.

Change Over Time   3

Essential Skill

Students can support in writing (both graphic organizer and narrative form) story or character changes in a story or across a series.

Materials

- Timeline drawn on chart paper labeled Beginning on the far left and End at the far right
- Several trade books demonstrating a clear character change (see Suggested Texts)

Figure 41. Character Change Timeline

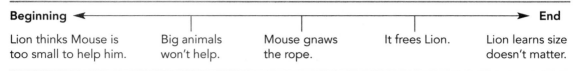

| Beginning ◀──▶ End |
| Lion thinks Mouse is too small to help him. | Big animals won't help. | Mouse gnaws the rope. | It frees Lion. | Lion learns size doesn't matter. |

Procedure

Modeling

1. Read a familiar story, preferably a folk tale with a clear character change such as *The Lion and the Mouse* (Watts, 2007). Then say, "Sometimes a character will change in a story, and if we understand why the character changes or how the character changes it helps us to understand the story better. In the story I just read I know that the lion changes what he thinks about the mouse in the story, but I need to find proof in the story to help me back up my thinking. I will use a timeline so you can see how I track my thinking." Draw a timeline on chart paper, labeling the far left side Beginning and the far right side End. Write a short statement about what the character is thinking at the beginning of the story and what the character is thinking at the end of the story. For example, under Beginning on the timeline write, "The lion thinks the mouse is too small to help him." At the end of the timeline write, "The lion knows the mouse can help him, and he realizes the mouse's size doesn't matter." Then point out several details in the story that are causative actions precipitating the character's change. Write the actions under the lines drawn on the timeline (see Figure 41).

2. Under the timeline write the following question: "How does the lion change from the beginning of the story to the end? Give details from the story to support your answer." Then say, "Today I am going to write about the answer to this question, using the timeline to help me remember the details that support my thinking." Write the following brief response:

> In the story *The Lion and the Mouse*, the lion changes his thinking about the mouse. At the beginning the lion thinks the mouse is too small to help him. The big animals wouldn't help him get out of the trap so when the mouse came along the lion didn't think he could help because he was too small. The mouse bit the ropes and let the lion out. At the end the lion learned the mouse's size didn't matter.

Guided Reading

3. Read another folk tale aloud and then draw a new timeline. Elicit responses from the class about how the character was at the beginning and then how the character was at the end of the story. Ask for events in the story that precip-

itate the change and write them on the timeline. Finally, with students craft a narrative response explaining how the character changes.

4. Repeat this lesson several times during small-group guided reading, eliminating the use of the timeline and moving to an oral discussion of character change. Then ask students to individually write a brief narrative explaining the change.

Independent Reading

5. Ask students to create a timeline and craft a written response about character change while working in small groups or with partners and using a self-selected text.

Follow-Up Activities

• Periodically have students respond to the following question after completing an independent reading book: "How does the main character in the story change from the beginning of the story until the end?" Give details to support your answer.

• Introduce how to use a character map or any other graphic organizer to demonstrate change over time.

• Repeat the discussion of change over time, using series books and examining character change across series.

Assessment

Students will be able to recognize events in a story that cause character change and be able to write a short narrative explaining the change.

• After a guided reading session, use the prompt provided in the follow-up mini-lessons section. Ask students to write a short narrative explaining character change. Individually confer with each student, checking for understanding and accuracy.

Suggested Texts

Bunting, E. (1999). *Smoky night*. San Diego, CA: Harcourt.

Friedman, I.R. (1987). *How my parents learned to eat*. Boston: Houghton Mifflin.

Johnston, T. (1994). *Amber on the mountain*. New York: Penguin.

Polacco, P. (1995). *Babushka's doll*. New York: Simon & Schuster.

Polacco, P. (1998). *Thank you, Mr. Falker*. New York: Penguin.

Watts, B. (2007). *The lion and the mouse: A fable by Aesop*. New York: North-South Books.

Essential Skill

Students will read across texts and use prior experiences (schema) to recognize, predict, and comprehend different genres.

Materials

- Four-column chart on chart paper, with columns labeled Genre, Language, Characteristics, and Title
- Blank Characteristics of Genre charts—one for each student
- Trade books written in various genres—folk tale/fable, poetry, mystery, non-fiction, historical fiction (see Suggested Texts)

Procedure

Modeling

1. Create a four-column chart with columns labeled Genre, Characteristics, Language, and Titles. Write the following genres in column one: Poetry, Mystery, Nonfiction, and Historical Fiction (other genres should be added throughout the year). Review the concept that each genre has certain things that make it special. These special qualities are called the characteristics of the genre. Say, "These characteristics allow us to recognize what genre we are reading. Knowing about genre can help us clear up any confusions we may have while reading. Also, learning these characteristics can help us write in some of these genres. For the next few weeks we are going to read in these genres in order to recognize the language and characteristics special to each of them." All of the genres listed on the Characteristics of Genre chart should be well represented during read-aloud time; focus exclusively on one genre per week. With each new genre introduced, discuss how to recognize the genre. As you cover each genre, have students help fill out the columns on the chart (see Figure 42).

Guided Reading

2. For guided reading choose books that match the focus genre for the week. Ask students to think about the characteristics and language of the genre, and add the titles to the chart with student input.

3. Give each student a blank Characteristics of Genre chart (see Appendix A). Scaffold student learning as they fill in the chart after each guided reading selection.

Figure 42. Characteristics of Genre Chart

Genre	Characteristics	Language of the Genre	Titles
Poetry	White space Line breaks	Similes and metaphors Unusual words	*Poetry from A to Z* (Janeczko, 1994) *When a City Leans Against the Sky* (DeFina, 1997)
Mystery	A problem is presented Clues are in the story The problem is solved	"Suddenly..." A lot of sequence words: *next, then, after*	*Grandpa's Teeth* (Clement, 1999) *Nate the Great and the Monster Mess* (Sharmat, 2001) *Art Dog* (Hurd, 1998)
Nonfiction	Facts around a topic Lots of illustrations or photographs	Factual language tied to the topic	*How a Book Is Made* (Aliki, 1988) *Why Do Dogs Bark?* (Holub, 2001)
Historical fiction	Story elements can be real Setting is usually important to the story	Biographical words: born, *married, died* Family words	*Sam the Minuteman* (Benchley, 1987) *Tonight on the* Titanic (Osborne, 1999) *A Picnic in October* (Bunting, 1999)

Independent Reading

4. Throughout the year have students read extensively in a number of genres, filling in the Characteristics of Genre charts they started during guided reading with information for their self-selected titles.

5. Have students indicate genre next to titles on their reading logs. Every few weeks ask students to graph the titles on their log by genre to see if they need to read more in a particular genre (see Figure 43).

Follow-Up Activities

• Have students add books to the initial genres listed on the chart. The titles will be generated from their independent reading or guided reading. Students can also recommend adding other genres to the chart; however, if they would like to add a new genre, it should be introduced to the entire class during a shared reading session.

• Along with students, sort through the classroom library and assemble genre baskets. Place these in a prominent place in the library.

Figure 43. Reading Graph by Genre

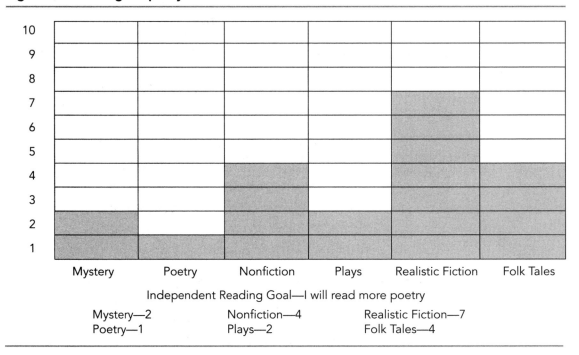

Independent Reading Goal—I will read more poetry

Mystery—2	Nonfiction—4	Realistic Fiction—7
Poetry—1	Plays—2	Folk Tales—4

• Introduce and have students write in different genres—especially nonfiction and poetry—during writers' workshop.

Assessment

Students will demonstrate the ability to identify the genre of a book and name some of its characteristics.

• During independent reading conferences, ask students to name the genre of the book they are reading and to support their answer by pointing out some of the characteristics aligned with that genre.

Suggested Texts

Poetry

DeFina, A.A. (1997). *When a city leans against the sky*. Honesdale, PA: Boyds Mills Press.

Janeczko, P.B. (1994). *Poetry from A to Z: A guide for young writers*. New York: Simon & Schuster.

Nonfiction

Aliki. (1988). *How a book is made.* New York: HarperCollins.

Holub, J. (2001). *Why do dogs bark?* New York: Dial Books for Young Readers.

Locker, T. (2001). *Sky tree: Seeing science through art.* New York: HarperCollins.

Mystery

Clement, R. (1999). *Grandpa's teeth.* New York: HarperCollins.

Hurd, T. (1998). *Art dog.* New York: HarperCollins.

Sharmat, M. (2001). *Nate the great and the monster mess.* New York: Random House.

Historical Fiction

Benchley, N. (1987). *Sam the minuteman.* New York: HarperCollins.

Bunting, E. (1999). *A picnic in October.* San Diego, CA: Harcourt.

Osborne, M.P. (1999). *Tonight on the* Titanic. New York: Random House.

Compare/Contrast/Conclude

5

Essential Skill

Students will be able to support an opinion or answer a question in written form using knowledge of the similarities and differences between texts.

Materials

• Two short texts, such as an article and a story, written on the same topic (see Suggested Texts)

• T-chart drawn on chart paper

Procedure

Modeling

1. Read two short texts on the same topic (preferably an informational article and a short story or poem). Then draw a T-chart on the board and explain that based on the information you have read in the two pieces of text you have learned something or formed an opinion. For example, read two texts about buffalo. Then say, "Before I read these two stories I believed that buffalo were mean, useless animals, but now I believe they can be very useful." Continue by saying, "My new thinking is an opinion I formed about the topic I just read about, but I need to find information in the two pieces of text to back up my thinking." At the top of the T-chart write a statement such

as, I think buffalo are very useful animals. Label the first column Article and the second column Story. Then look through the article and, in numerical order, write the supportive information from the article in the left column. Next look through the story or poem for supportive information and list it in the right column. The evidence can be stated or inferential; however, if the evidence is inferred, explain the thinking to the class. (If possible align the information in corresponding order in each of the columns. However, explain that one source may contain more information than another so one column may be longer and contain more information.) After finding the information say, "After examining the article and story and finding evidence to support my opinion, I can conclude my opinion is a good one." Then explain to the class that if you had to write about the opinion you formed from reading the two pieces, the T-chart would help you to supply and organize the necessary proof.

2. Read two short pieces of text on a similar topic, such as school safety, and then state that sometimes we need to answer a question, compose a letter, or write a report using information from more than one source. Explain that planning with a T-chart helps to organize the information we might need to support our writing. For example, write a letter to the principal explaining why you think your school should have an assembly about playground safety. Then proceed as in the previous lesson, finding information from the two texts and charting it in the two columns to support your request. Follow up by using the information to write an persuasive letter.

Guided Reading

3. Write the following question on the board: "Do you think children should have pets?" Read two texts about children and pets. After reading the texts, create two T-charts, one with a positive opinion about having pets and one with a negative opinion about having pets. After eliciting information based on the texts from students and writing it on the two T-charts, ask students to choose the opinion they want to support. Using the information on the T-charts, ask students to write individual opinion pieces to answer the prompt on the board. This lesson will allow students to see that different opinions can be formed from the same information and all opinions are valid when supported by information in the text.

Independent Reading

4. Have students support an opinion or write a report about a specific topic discussed during science or another other subject area. For example, ask students to answer the question, "How did dinosaurs become extinct?" Have

students use a T-chart for planning and two sources of information to get evidence to support their opinion. Make sure students select topics with enough classroom material (both fiction and nonfiction texts) available for the research and writing.

Follow-Up Activities

• Model how to plan and use information from various fiction and nonfiction sources throughout the year. Background information should be used to write letters, answer questions, or write brief reports or articles on a focused topic such as, "Should school lunchrooms serve only healthy snacks?"

• Repeat these lessons, using different types of texts and writing in different genres, such as letters supporting a certain idea or an article for the school newspaper asking people to get involved with a certain issue.

Assessment

Students will be able to select, plan, and write informative pieces based on information from two or more texts.

• After students have read two short pieces of text during shared or guided reading, ask them to respond to a prompt that will require them to select, plan, and write an informative piece based on information they have gathered from two texts. Assess the piece, making sure the students used information from both texts.

Suggested Texts

Books

Branley, F. (1991). *What happened to the dinosaurs?* New York: HarperCollins.

Carrick, C. (1985). *Patrick's dinosaurs.* Boston: Houghton Mifflin.

Cherry, L.(2001). *The shaman's apprentice.* San Diego, CA. Harcourt.

Ringgold, F (1996). *Tar beach.* New York: Random House.

Simon, S. (2005). *Skyscrapers.* New York: Chronicle Books.

Stille, D.(2000). *Tropical rainforests.* New York: Scholastic.

Magazines

Kids discover. New York: Kids Discover.

Ranger Rick. Reston, VA: National Wildlife Federation.

Sports illustrated for kids. New York: Time.

Time for kids. New York: Time.

Essential Skill

Students will be able to recognize the main idea in a story and support it with details both in oral and written form.

Materials

• Several narrative texts (see Suggested Texts)
• Story web (see Appendix A)

Procedure

Modeling

1. Choose a narrative text and say to the class, "When we read a story, in order to know what the story is about we need to fit the pieces of the story together inside our head so we can see the whole picture. It is just like putting the pieces of a puzzle together. The main idea is the whole picture the author wants us to recognize. The details are like the pieces of the puzzle the author puts in the story to help make the picture or the main idea in our minds. Continue by saying, "Remember when we read *The Lion and the Mouse*? Today, I'm going to reread it, and when I finish I will tell you what I think the story is about or what the main idea is and the details that I think are the proof or evidence to support my thinking." Proceed by reading the complete story and at the conclusion say, "I think the main idea in this story is that size doesn't matter but thinking through a problem does." Return to the story and point out the details serving as evidence to support the main idea. Point out how paying attention to the end of the story (the resolution) or how the problem was solved helped to formulate the main idea in your head.

2. On the following day say, "Today I am going to show you how I put my thinking about the main idea and my supporting evidence from the story into a story web that can help us organize our ideas in case we have to summarize or answer questions about the story." Draw a large circle on chart paper and then draw three descending circles from the main circle. Label the three descending circles Beginning, Middle, and End. Then say, "I am going to put the main idea or what the story is mostly about into the main circle and I will label it Main Idea. This idea forms in your head after you put the events of the story together. These events, or evidence, are what I am going to write in these other circles to prove my thinking is correct." Return to each section of the

story and record the major events in the small circles. Finally, summarize the story orally using the story web as a guide.

3. Repeat the lesson using a different story, demonstrating how to fill in a story web and then how to write a summary using the story web as a guide.

Guided Reading

4. Read a story aloud and ask students to identify the main idea and the supporting details.

5. Create a story web together, filling in the main idea and supporting details.

6. Along with students, write a summary using the read-aloud story. Refer back to the story web for support.

Independent Reading

7. After completing an independent reading book, have students fill in a story web (see Appendix A), and summarize the book.

Follow-Up Activities

• During subsequent lessons, model how to use the story web as a guide to formulate a short written response to the following questions:

What is this story mostly about?

What is a good title for this story?

What lesson did you learn from this story?

What is the main idea of this story?

The answer to the question will go in the main circle, and the details or proof will go in the lower circles.

• During guided reading, assign partners from within each group to either create a story web and summarize the story or create a story web and answer a question relating to the story read aloud.

• After completing an independent reading book, have students answer questions related to the main idea by using a story web to plan their answer.

Assessment

Students will be able to identify the main idea of a story and support their thinking both orally and in writing with details.

• At the completion of a guided reading session, write on the board "What is the main idea of this story?" Ask students to write a brief summary answering the question. After they are finished, confer with them during independent reading time and ask them to explain their answer. Assess the response according to the accuracy of the supportive details the child selects from the book.

Suggested Texts

Mills, L.A. (1991). *The rag coat.* Boston: Little, Brown.

Steig, W. (1988). *Brave Irene.* New York: Farrar, Straus and Giroux.

Stock, C. (1993). *Where are you going, Manyoni?* New York: HarperCollins.

Ward, H. (2003). *The tin forest.* New York: Penguin.

Woodson, J. (2001). *The other side.* New York: Penguin.

Reproducibles

Blank Letter Template

[Date]_____

[Greeting]

[Body]

_____

_____

_____

_____

_____

_____

_____

[Closing]

[Name]

Book Recommendation Form

Recommended by:

Title and author of the book:

Genre:

Short summary of the book (4–5 sentences):

What is your opinion of the book? Would you recommend the book or not? Why?

Change Over Time Organizer

Name _____   Date _____

Title _____

Author _____

Character _____

Beginning _____

Event
Event
Event

End _____

Character Web

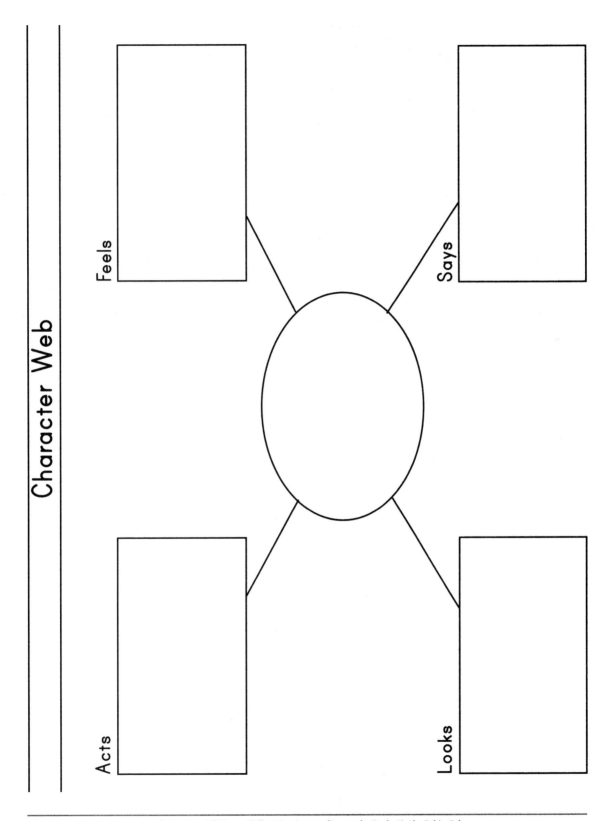

Feels

Says

Acts

Looks

Characteristics of Genre Chart

Genre	Characteristics	Language	Titles
Poetry			
Mystery			
Nonfiction			
Historical fiction			

EVENT

Description
of Event

Date:

Time:

Place:

Grocery List Template

CANNED FOODS

MEAT AND POULTRY

_____

_____

_____

_____

_____

_____

SNACKS

DRINKS

_____

_____

_____

_____

_____

_____

FRUITS AND
VEGETABLES

DESSERTS

_____

_____

_____

_____

_____

_____

Heart Map

Heart Map (Sectioned)

You Are Invited...

List Paper

_____

_____

_____

_____

_____

_____

_____

_____

_____

_____

_____

_____

Main Idea Summary Sheet

Name _____ Date _____

Title _____

This book is mostly about _____

_____

_____

I know this because in the beginning _____

_____

_____

_____

In the middle _____

_____

_____

In the end _____

_____

_____

My Memory Paper

My Memory Paper

Postcard Template

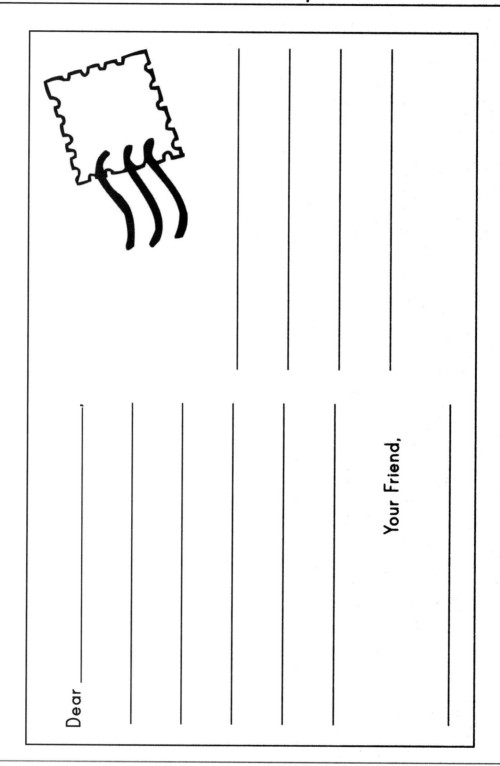

Dear _____

Your Friend,

Sample Letter

Dear Sam,

    I got a new dog. We call him Boots. We gave him this name because he is white with black paws.

    He likes to run and run. He likes to bite things. He likes to rip up paper.

    I hope you can come and see him soon. You will like him.

                   Your friend,

                   Tim

Sample Letter for Assessment

Dear Emma,

    I went to the park today. I love to go on the swings. I can swing way up high. I also like to go on the slide. I slide down very fast. It is fun to slide down fast. I took my doll to the park. I put her on the swing and pushed her down the slide.

    I want you to come to see me. We can go to the park together. That would be the most fun.

Your friend,

Susan

Developing Essential Literacy Skills: A Continuum of Lessons for Grades K–3 by Robin Cohen.
© 2008 by the International Reading Association. May be copied for classroom use.

Setting Map

Name _____ Date _____

SETTING

The story setting is where the action takes place in the story (at school, at a football game, in the woods, and so on).

Select a book. Title _____

Author/Illustrator _____

* Draw the different settings where the action takes place in the story.
* Draw as many details as you can to illustrate your settings.

Beginning Setting	Middle Setting	End Setting

Story Elements Chart

Name _____ Date _____

Title _____

Author _____

Characters	Setting	Events

Story Frame 1

Name _____ Date _____

Title _____

Author _____

In this story the main character is _____.

The problem starts when _____

_____.

After that, _____

_____.

Next _____

_____.

Then _____

_____.

The problem is solved when _____

_____.

Story Frame 2

Name _____ Date _____

Title _____

Author _____

At the beginning of the story _____ is _____.

Then _____

_____

_____

_____

happens. Next _____

_____ happens and finally _____

happens. At the end of the story _____

_____ is _____.

Story Frame 3

Name _____ Date _____

Title _____

This story begins when _____

_____ .

The problem is _____

_____ .

The next thing that happens is_____

_____ .

Then _____

_____ .

After that, _____

_____ .

The problem is solved when _____

_____ .

Story Map 1

Name _____ Date _____

Title _____

Beginning

$\Downarrow$

Middle

$\Downarrow$

End

Story Map 2

Name _____ Date _____

Title _____

Setting

```
┌─────────────────────────────────────────────────────────┐
│                                                         │
│                                                         │
│                                                         │
│                                                         │
│                                                         │
└─────────────────────────────────────────────────────────┘
```

Characters _____   _____

_____   _____

_____   _____

Problem

```
┌─────────────────────────────────────────────────────────┐
│                                                         │
│                                                         │
│                                                         │
│                                                         │
│                                                         │
└─────────────────────────────────────────────────────────┘
```

Event 1 _____

Event 2 _____

Event 3 _____

Solution

```
┌─────────────────────────────────────────────────────────┐
│                                                         │
│                                                         │
│                                                         │
│                                                         │
│                                                         │
└─────────────────────────────────────────────────────────┘
```

Story Retelling Chart

Name _____ Date _____

Title:		
This story is mostly about		
Beginning	Middle	End

Story Structure Boxes

Name _____ Date _____

Title

Beginning   Middle   End

Story Web

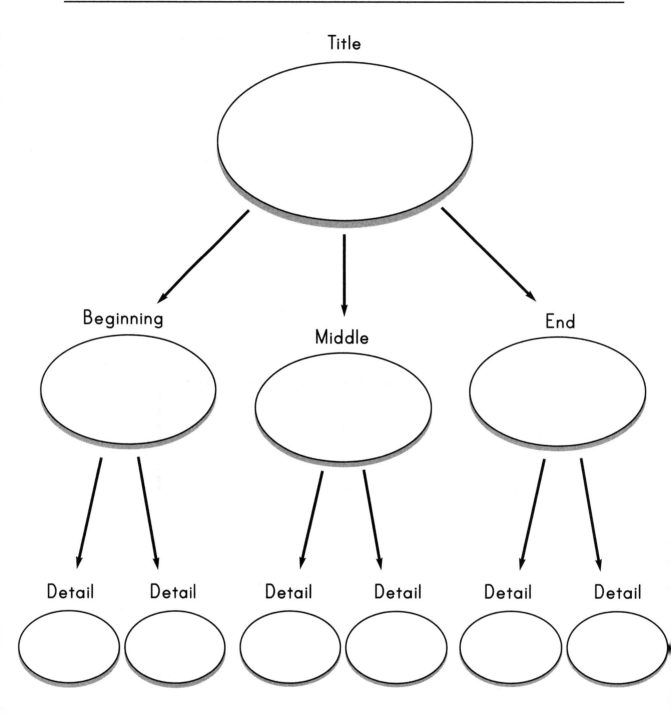

Title

Beginning

Middle

End

Detail   Detail   Detail   Detail   Detail   Detail

T-Chart

Name _____ Date _____

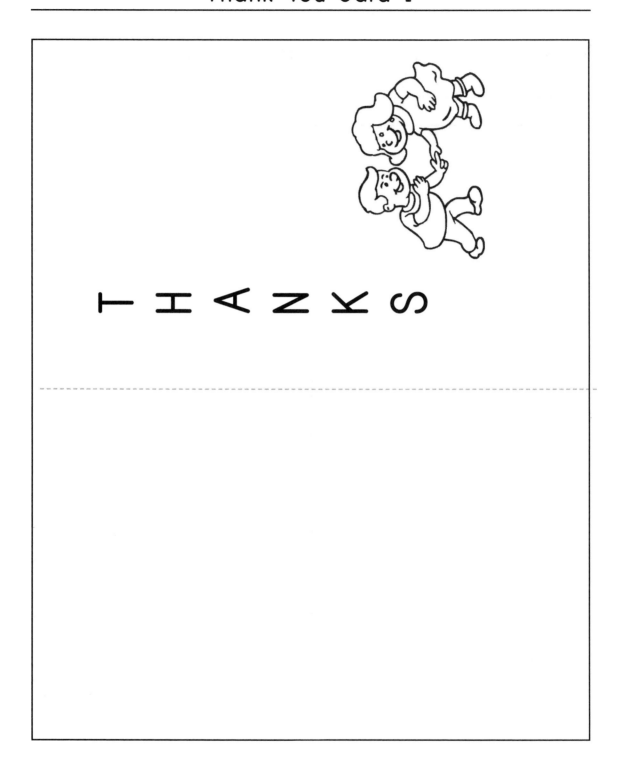

THANKS

THANKS

Venn Diagram

Name _____ Date _____

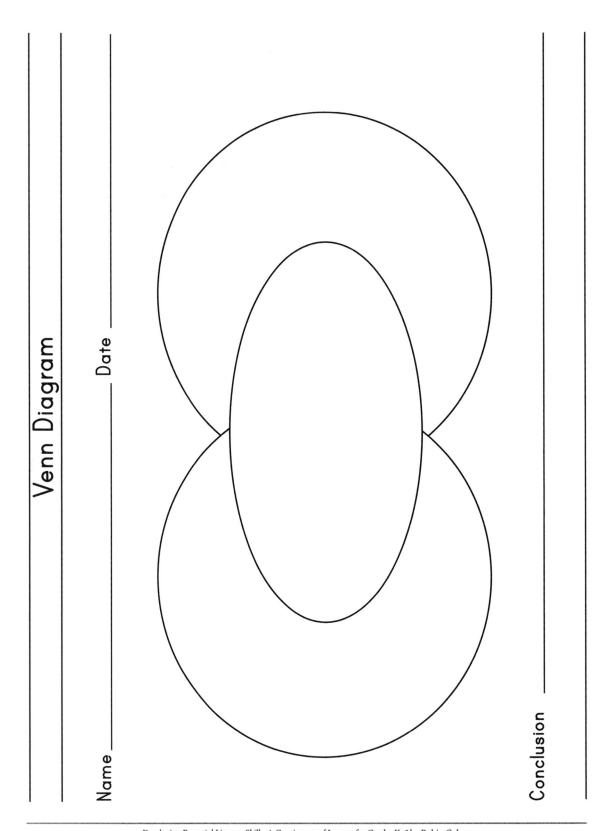

Conclusion _____

Writing Ideas

Name _____ Date _____

Y-Chart

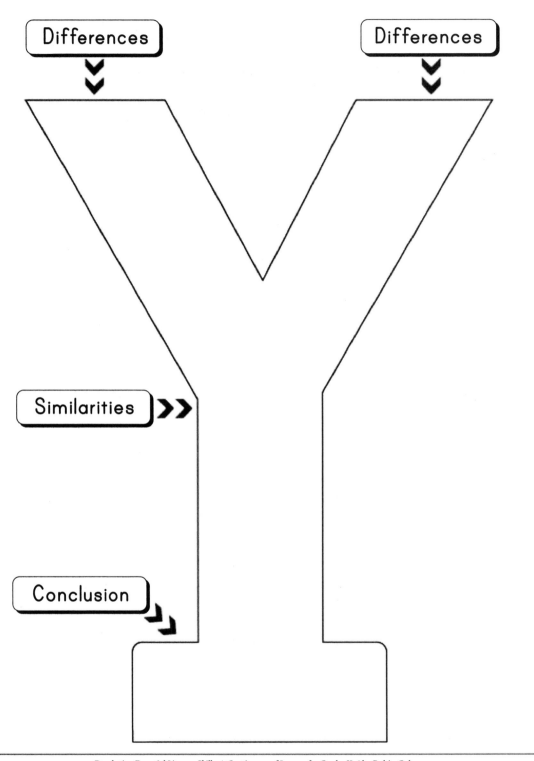

Differences

Differences

Similarities

Conclusion

Additional Resources: Checklists, Word Lists, Reading Logs, and Rubrics

Grade 1 Editing Checklist

1, _____ I have read my writing again.

4 _____ All my sentences begin with capital letters.

5 _____ All names start with a capital letter.

5, _____ All my sentences end with a period (.) or question mark (?) or exclamation point (!).

6, _____ I have used the word wall to check my words.

_____ I have circled words that don't look right.

2, _____ I left spaces between my words.

3. _____ I wrote neatly.

_____ My story has a beginning, a middle, and an end.

Adapted from Fry, E.B., & Kress, J.E. (2006). *The reading teacher's book of lists* (5th ed.). San Francisco: Jossey-Bass.

Grade 2 Editing Checklist

_____ I reread my piece to be sure it makes sense.

_____ I capitalized the first letter in every sentence.

_____ I capitalized all names.

_____ I capitalized the letter "I" when I'm talking about myself.

_____ All my sentences have an end mark—period, question mark, or exclamation point.

_____ I checked the word wall for correct spelling.

_____ I circled all the words I was not sure how to spell.

_____ I wrote neatly.

_____ I indented each new paragraph.

_____ I have an ending sentence.

Adapted from Fry, E.B., & Kress, J.E. (2006). *The reading teacher's book of lists* (5th ed.). San Francisco: Jossey-Bass.

Developing Essential Literacy Skills: A Continuum of Lessons for Grades K–3 by Robin Cohen.
© 2008 by the International Reading Association. May be copied for classroom use.

Grade 3 Editing Checklist

_____ All sentences begin with a capital letter.

_____ All people's names and the names of places, countries, cities, days of the week, and months have capital letters.

_____ Each sentence ends with a period, question mark, or exclamation point.

_____ Paragraphs are indented.

_____ All spelling has been checked with the word wall, the dictionary, or my editing partner.

_____ The opening sentence is interesting.

_____ The piece has an ending sentence.

_____ Quotation marks were used when talking took place.

Adapted from Fry, E.B., & Kress, J.E. (2006). *The reading teacher's book of lists* (5th ed.). San Francisco: Jossey-Bass.

Kindergarten High-Frequency Word List

a	I	my
am	in	on
and	is	see
at	it	the
come	like	this
go	look	we
here	me	

Grade 1 High-Frequency Word List

A
a
about
after
all
am
an
and
are
as
at

B
back
be
because
been
big
but
by

C
came
can
come
could

D
day

did
do
down

F
first
for
from

G
get
go
going
got

H
had
has
have
he
her
here
him
his

I
I
if
in

into
is
it

J
just

L
like
little
look

M
made
make
me
more
my

N
no
not
now

O
of
off
on
one

only
or
our
out
over

S
said
saw
see
she
so
some

T
that
the
their
them
then
there
they
this
to
two

U
up

V
very

W
was
we
well
went
were
what
when
where
which
who
will
with
would

Y
you
your

Adapted from Fry, E.B., & Kress, J.E. (2006). *The reading teacher's book of lists* (5th ed.). San Francisco: Jossey-Bass.

Grade 2 High-Frequency Word List

always	girl	name	take
again	give	need	tell
air	good	new	than
also	great	number	these
animal	help	oil	thing
another	high	old	think
any	home	other	three
ask	house	page	through
around	how	part	time
away	kind	people	too
answer	know	picture	try
before	large	place	turn
boy	learn	play	us
call	letter	point	use
children	line	put	walk
city	live	read	want
different	long	right	water
does	many	same	way
each	may	sentence	why
end	mean	set	word
even	most	should	work
every	mother	show	world
farm	move	small	write
father	much	sound	year
find	must	spell	such

Grade 3 High-Frequency Word List

above	eat	keep	ten
add	early	later	thank
afternoon	eight	leave	third
almost	enough	let	those
along	eyes	longer	though
always	face	love	today
bed	fall	might	together
began	family	myself	took
begin	far	near	town
beginning	fast	never	turn
below	few	next	
between	fine	night	under
book	fly	often	until
both	food	once	upon
	friend	open	warm
car	funny	ride	watch
carry	gave	round	water
city	goes	second	while
close	grow	seem	without
cold	happy	sister	woman
country	hard	sleep	write
cut	hear	sometimes	
	hope	something	yellow
didn't	hot	soon	yes
don't	it's	start	yesterday
door	important	stop	
	jump		

Adapted from Fry, E.B., & Kress, J.E. (2006). *The reading teacher's book of lists* (5th ed.). San Francisco: Jossey-Bass.

Kindergarten Reading Log

Name _____ Class _____

#	Date	Title and Author	Type of Text F = Fiction N = Nonfiction P = Poetry	My Opinion 😊 😐 ☹️

Developing Essential Literacy Skills: A Continuum of Lessons for Grades K–3 by Robin Cohen.
© 2008 by the International Reading Association. May be copied for classroom use.

Grade 1 Reading Log

Name _____ Class _____

#	Date	Title and Author	Type of Text F = Fiction N = Nonfiction P = Poetry	My Opinion 😊 😐 ☹️

Grade 2 Reading Log

Name _____

Class _____

#	Date	Title and Author	Type of Text F = Fiction (What type?) N = Nonfiction P = Poetry	I Read This Book 1 = Alone 2 = With an Adult 3 = With a Partner or Group	Reading This Book Was 1 = Easy 2 = Just Right 3 = Hard	My Opinion 1 = Didn't Like 2 = Okay 3 = Good 4 = Great

Grade 3 Reading Log

Name _____

Class _____

Key

F = Fiction (What type?) NF = Nonfiction
P = Poetry
E = Easy   JR = Just Right   C = Challenge

#	Date	Title	Author	Genre	E, JR, C	If Abandoned, What Was Your Reason for Abandoning the Book?

Retelling Rubric (Grades K–3)

Skill	Not at All	Some of the Time	Most of the Time	All of the Time
The story is structured around a beginning, a middle, and an end.				
The most essential parts of the story were chosen to retell.				
Important details are included.				
Multiple sentences are used to tell a story.				
Story elements (characters' names, setting, and events) are included and correct.				
Interesting language, humor, emotions, details, sounds, or movement are included.				
The retell makes sense.				

Personal Narrative Writing Rubric (Grades 1–3)

Skill	1 Not Evident	2 Evident Some of the Time	3 Evident Most of the Time	4 Evident All of the Time
The story has a beginning, a middle, and an end.				
The story has a main focus and supporting details.				
Events in the story are sequenced in correct order.				
Sentences and names begin with capital letters.				
Correct punctuation (periods, question marks, exclamation points) is used.				
Word choice is interesting and varied.				
High-frequency words are spelled correctly.				
Sentences are complete and varied.				

Friendly Letter Writing Rubric (Grades 1–3)

Skill	1 Not Evident	2 Evident Some of the Time	3 Evident Most of the Time	4 Evident All of the Time
The essential parts of a friendly letter are included: date, opening (greeting), body, closing, and name.				
The purpose for writing is clear and to the point.				
The letter contains interesting details.				
Word choice is interesting and varied.				
Sentences are complete and varied.				
Correct punctuation is used (periods, question marks, exclamation points).				
Sentences and names begin with capital letters as well as the greeting and closing.				
High-frequency words are spelled correctly.				

Additional Text Resources to Support Units of Study

Text Structure

Kindergarten

Katz, K. (2001). *Counting kisses.* New York: Simon & Schuster.

Leopold, N.C. (2002). *K is for kitten.* New York: Penguin.

Williams, V.B. (2004). *Amber was brave, Essie was smart.* New York: HarperCollins.

Grade 1

Butterworth, N. (2003). *My grandma is wonderful.* Cambridge, MA: Candlewick.

Godwin, L. (2002). *Central Park serenade.* New York: HarperCollins.

Grade 2

Lasky, K. (1996). *A journey to the new world: The diary of Remember Patience Whipple.* New York: Scholastic.

Mannis, C.D. (2002). *One leaf rides the wind: Counting in a Japanese garden.* New York: Viking Press.

Schaeffer, C.L. (1999). *The squiggle.* New York: Bantam Dell.

Grade 3

Garza, C.L. (2005). *Family pictures.* San Francisco: Children's Book Press.

Pratt, K.J. (1992). *A walk in the rainforest.* Nevada City, CA: Dawn.

Raven, M.T. (2002). *M is for Mayflower: A Massachusetts alphabet.* Chelsea, MI: Sleeping Bear Press.

Characteristics of Genre

Kindergarten

Ada, A.F. (2001). *Gathering the sun: An alphabet in Spanish and English*. New York: HarperCollins.

Brown, M. (1997). *Stone soup*. New York: Simon & Schuster.

Morris, A. (1994). *Loving*. New York: HarperCollins.

Shannon, D. (2004). *Alice the fairy*. New York: Scholastic.

Grade 1

Hudson, C.W. (1990). *Bright eyes, brown skin*. Orange, NJ: Just Us Books.

Kalman, B. (1999). *What is a reptile?* New York: Crabtree.

Rau, D.M. (2004). *Jump rope*. Minnetonka, MN: Capstone.

Grade 2

Benchley, N. (1987). *Sam the minuteman*. New York: HarperCollins.

Brett, J. (1989). *The mitten*. New York: HarperCollins.

Davies, N. (2000). *Big blue whale*. Cambridge, MA: Candlewick.

dePaola, T. (1997). *Jamie O'Rourke and the big potato*. New York: Penguin.

Long, M. (2003). *How I became a pirate*. San Diego, CA: Harcourt.

Tucker, K. (2003). *The seven Chinese sisters*. Chicago: Albert Whitman.

Grade 3

Benchley, N. (1987). *Sam the minuteman*. New York: HarperCollins.

Berger, M. (1998). *Chirping crickets*. New York: HarperCollins.

Brown, M. (1998). *Arthur accused!* Boston: Little, Brown.

Clement, R. (1999). *Grandpa's teeth*. New York: HarperCollins.

Hurd, T. (1998). *Art dog*. New York: HarperCollins.

Locker, T. (2002). *Water dance*. San Diego, CA: Harcourt.

Osborne, M.P. (1999). *Tonight on the* Titanic. New York: Random House.

Sharmat, M. (2001). *Nate the great and the monster mess*. New York: Random House.

Whalen, G. (1997). *The Indian school*. New York: HarperCollins.

Story Elements: Character

Kindergarten

Bridwell, N. (2004). *Clifford's first sleepover*. New York: Scholastic.

Capucilli, A.S. (2005). *Biscuit wins a prize*. New York: HarperCollins.

Cousins, L. (2002). *Maisy cleans up*. Cambridge, MA: Candlewick.

Kirk, D. (1997). *Miss Spider's new car*. New York: Scholastic.

Grade 1

Cosby, B. (1998). *Shipwreck Saturday*. New York: Scholastic.

dePaola, T. (2003). *Strega Nona takes a vacation*. New York: Penguin.

Gantos, J. (1980). *Rotten Ralph*. Boston: Houghton Mifflin.

Schachner, J.B. (2003). *Skippyjon Jones*. New York: Penguin.

Grade 2

Aardema, V. (2000). *Anansi does the impossible! An Ashanti tale*. New York: Aladdin.

Cazet, D. (2004). *Minnie and Moo: Night of the living bed*. New York: HarperCollins.

Parish, P. (2005). *Amelia Bedelia helps out*. New York: HarperCollins.

Rylant, C. (2005). *Henry and Mudge and the funny lunch*. New York: Simon & Schuster.

Grade 3

Brown, J. (2003). *Stanley in space*. New York: HarperCollins.

Lindgren, A. (1977). *Pippi goes on board*. New York: Penguin.

Lindgren, A. (1977). *Pippi Longstockings*. New York: Penguin.

Stilton, G. (2005). *Watch your whiskers, Stilton!* New York: HarperCollins.

Story Elements: Setting

Kindergarten

Alborough, J. (2002). *Hug.* Cambridge, MA: Candlewick.

Day, A. (1997). *Good dog, Carl.* New York: Simon & Schuster.

Lewis, K. (1999). *Chugga-chugga choo-choo.* New York: Hyperion Books for Children.

Raffi. (1992). *Baby beluga.* New York: Crown.

Grade 1

Fox, M. (2005). *Hunwick's egg.* San Diego, CA: Harcourt.

Ho, M. (2000). *Hush! A Thai lullaby.* New York: Scholastic.

Lester, H. (1990). *Tacky the penguin.* Boston: Houghton Mifflin.

Miranda, A. (1997). *To market, to market.* San Diego, CA: Harcourt.

Grade 2

Brett, J. (2004). *Armadillo rodeo.* New York: Penguin.

Brett, J. (2004). *The umbrella.* New York: Penguin.

Lithgow, J. (2005). *Micawber.* New York: Simon & Schuster.

Zolotow, C. (1994). *The seashore book.* New York: HarperCollins.

Grade 3

Polacco, P. (2004). *John Phillip Duck.* New York: Penguin.

Pratt, K. (1992). *A walk in the rainforest.* Nevada City, CA: Dawn.

Wood, D. (2005). *Quiet place.* New York: Aladdin.

Yashima, T. (1976). *Crow boy.* New York: Penguin.

REFERENCES

Anderson, R.C., Hiebert, E.H., Scott, J.A., & Wilkinson, I.A.G. (1985). *Becoming a nation of readers: The report of the Commission on Reading.* Washington, DC: National Institute of Education.

Anderson, R.C., Wilson, P., & Fielding, L. (1988). Growth in reading and how children spend their time outside of school. *Reading Research Quarterly, 23,* 285–303.

Blanton, W.E., & Wood, K.D. (1984). Direct instruction in reading comprehension test-taking skill. *Reading World, 24,* 10–19.

Calkins, L.M. (1994). *The art of teaching writing.* Portsmouth, NH: Heinemann.

Calkins, L.M. (2001). *The art of teaching reading.* New York: Addison-Wesley.

Cowen, J.E. (2003). *A balanced approach to beginning reading instruction.* Newark, DE: International Reading Association.

Cunningham, P.M. (2000). *Phonics they use: Words for reading and writing* (3rd ed.). New York: Longman.

Cunningham, P.M., & Allington, R.L. (1999). *Classrooms that work: They can all read and write* (2nd ed.). New York: Longman.

Cunningham, P.M., & Hall, D.P. (1998). *Month-by-month phonics: A second chance for struggling readers and students learning English.* Greensboro, NC: Carson Dellosa Publishing.

Duffy, G.G., Roehler, L.R., Sivan, E., Rackliffe, G., Book, C., Meloth, M.S., et al. (1987). Effects of explaining the reasoning associated with using reading strategies. *Reading Research Quarterly, 23,* 347–368.

Duke, N.K., & Pearson, P.D. (2002). Effective practices for developing reading comprehension. In A.E. Farstrup & S.J. Samuels (Eds.), *What research has to say about reading instruction* (3rd ed., pp. 205–242). Newark, DE: International Reading Association.

Fletcher, R. (1996). *A writer's notebook: Unlocking the writer within you.* New York: HarperCollins.

Fletcher, R. (1999). *Live writing: Breathing life into your words.* New York: HarperCollins.

Fletcher, R. (2000). *How writers work: Finding a process that works for you.* New York: HarperCollins.

Fountas, I.C., & Pinnell, G.S. (1996). *Guided reading: Good first teaching for all children.* Portsmouth, NH: Heinemann.

Fountas, I.C., & Pinnell, G.S. (1998). *Word matters: Teaching phonics and spelling in the reading/writing classroom.* Portsmouth, NH: Heinemann.

Fountas, I.C., & Pinnell, G.S. (1999). *Matching books to readers: Using leveled books in guided reading, K–3.* Portsmouth, NH: Heinemann.

Fountas, I.C., & Pinnell, G.S. (2000). *Guiding readers and writers: Grades 3–6.* Portsmouth, NH: Heinemann.

Fountas, I.C., & Pinnell, G.S. (2001). *Leveled books for readers, grades 3–6.* Portsmouth, NH: Heinemann.

Fry, E.B., & Kress, J.E. (2006). *The reading teacher's book of lists* (5th ed.). San Francisco: Jossey-Bass.

Gentry, J.R. (2000). *The literacy map: Guiding children to where they need to be.* New York: Mondo.

Guthrie, J.T. (2002). Preparing students for high stakes testing in reading. In A.E. Farstrup & S.J. Samuels (Eds.), *What research has to say about reading instruction* (3rd ed., pp. 370–391). Newark, DE: International Reading Association.

Harvey, S., & Goudvis, A. (2000). *Strategies that work: Teaching comprehension to enhance understanding.* York, ME: Stenhouse.

Heard, G. (1999). *Awakening the heart.* Portsmouth, NH: Heinemann.

International Reading Association & National Association for the Education of Young Children. (1998). *Learning to read and write: Developmentally appropriate practices for young children* (Position statement). Newark, DE; Washington, DC: Authors.

International Reading Association & National Council of Teachers of English. (1996). *Standards for the English language arts.* Newark, DE; Urbana, IL: Authors.

Keene, E., & Zimmerman, S. (1997). *Mosaic of thought: Teaching comprehension in a reader's workshop.* Portsmouth, NH: Heinemann.

Miller, D. (2002). *Reading with meaning: Teaching comprehension in primary grades.* Portland, ME: Stenhouse.

National Institute of Child Health and Human Development. (2000). *Report of the National Reading Panel. Teaching children to read: An evidence-based assessment of the scientific research literature on reading and its implications for reading instruction* (NIH Publication No. 00-4769). Washington, DC: U.S. Government Printing Office.

National Research Council. (1998). *Preventing reading difficulties in young children.* Washington, DC: National Academy Press.

New Standards Primary Literacy Committee. (1999). *Reading grade by grade & writing: Primary literacy standards for kindergarten through third grade.* New York: Board of Education.

New York State Department of Education. (1996). *Learning standards for English language arts.* Albany: New York State Department of Education.

Palincsar, A.S., & Brown, A.L. (1984). Reciprocal teaching of comprehension-fostering and comprehension-monitoring activities. *Cognition and Instruction, 2,* 117–175.

Pearson, P.D., & Gallagher, M.C. (1983). The instruction of reading comprehension. *Contemporary Educational Psychology, 8,* 317–345.

Pressley, M. (1998). *Reading instruction that works: The case for balanced teaching.* New York: Guilford.

Pressley, M., Johnson, C.J., Symons, S., McGoldrick, J.A., & Kurita, J. (1989). Strategies that improve children's memory and comprehension of text. *The Elementary School Journal, 90,* 3–32.

Raphael, T.E. (1986). Teaching question/answer relationships, revisited. *The Reading Teacher, 39,* 388–400.

Ray, K.W. (2001). *The writing workshop working through the hard parts (and they are all hard parts).* Urbana, IL: National Council of Teachers of English.

Taberski, S. (2000). *On solid ground: Strategies for teaching reading K–3.* Portsmouth, NH: Heinemann.

INDEX

Note: Page numbers followed by *f*, *t*, or *r* indicate figures, tables, and reproducibles, respectively.

T–V

T-CHARTS, 155r; compare–contrast, 35, 35f, 63–64, 64f, 121–123; evidence of inquiry, 36, 36f, 37, 37f; opinion with supporting details, 93, 93f

TABERSKI, S., 6

TEAGUE, M., 59

TEXT SELECTION: recommendations for, 62–63, 80, 91–92, 121, 177–180

TEXT STRUCTURE. *See* story structure

THANK-YOU CARDS, 17–18, 42–43, 70, 156r–157r

TIMELINE: character change, 116, 116f; story, 30, 58, 59f

Venn diagram, 57, 158r

W

WATTS, B., 116

WILKINSON, I.A.G., 3

WILLIAMS, V.B., 102

WILSON, P., 3

WOOD, K.D., 4

WORD LISTS, HIGH-FREQUENCY: grade 1, 51, 166; grade 2, 72, 167; grade 3, 102, 168; kindergarten, 165

WORD WORK: in balanced literacy model, 5t

WORKSHOP-STYLE TEACHING, 4

WRITING: in balanced literacy model, 5t; essential skills in, 6–7; essential skills continuum for, 7–8; grade 1 units on, 42–52; grade 2 units on, 70–81; grade 3 units on, 100–108; idea sheet for, 22–23, 159r; kindergarten units on, 16–24; outcomes continuum in, 9t; study units in, 8–12, 12t

Y–Z

Y-CHART, 57, 160r

ZIMMERMANN, S., 6